Articulate Studio Cookbook

Create training courses with Articulate Studio's strong interactivity and rich content capabilities, all within the familiarity of Microsoft PowerPoint

Robert Kennedy III

PUBLISHING

BIRMINGHAM - MUMBAI

Articulate Studio Cookbook

First published: November 2012

Production Reference: 1121112

Published by Packt Publishing Ltd
Livery Place
35 Livery Street
Birmingham B3 2PB, UK

ISBN 978-1-84969-308-0

www.packtpub.com

Cover Image by Asher Wishkerman (wishkerman@hotmail.com)

Credits

Author

Robert Kennedy III

Reviewers

Eleanor Mante

Mary Pienzi

Acquisition Editor

Joanna Finchen

Lead Technical Editor

Kedar Bhat

Technical Editor

Devdutt Kulkarni

Copy Editor

Insiya Morbiwala

Project Coordinator

Vishal Bodwani

Proofreaders

Maria Gould

Bernadette Watkins

Indexer

Rekha Nair

Graphics

Valentina D'silva

Aditi Gajjar

Production Coordinator

Shantanu Zagade

Cover Work

Shantanu Zagade

About the Author

Robert Kennedy III is a former High School and College Educator turned Entrepreneur. He has owned web development and now e-learning/training companies, and has spent almost a decade as a trainer in topics ranging from music industry preparation to technology and learning. Currently, as the owner of RKCS Learning Solutions, Robert spends a great deal of time teaching others how to integrate technologies into their business workflow and training companies on how to develop effective learning modules for their employees.

Robert earned his Masters degree online through the University of Maryland University College and is currently completing his PhD in Educational Technology with Walden University. Although he was a former classroom teacher, he will tell you that online education saved his life.

He is an admitted tech lover; when not working, Robert spends his time playing with or catching up on the latest gadgets. Sites such as CNET, Tech Crunch, and Engadget are probably permanently burned into his screen at this point.

Robert grew up in Bronx, New York, and is therefore legally obligated to be a fan of the New York Yankees. He takes this obligation seriously and watches every Yankees' game on his phone, iPad, computer, or TV. He loves sports in general and can be found playing softball, golf, basketball, or bowling at any point during the year.

I'd like to thank some pretty important people, who have helped me with the production of this book through their time, their sacrifice, and their skill. I'm probably going to forget some names but I hope you'll simply attribute that to age rather than intent. Yeah, I'm getting older and I'm dealing with it. Anyway, on to the names, in no particular order, my wife, Nadia, my lovely kids (yes, this is partly what daddy does when he is in the home office), my parents, Robert and Seslie, and some other really important people, Tom Kuhlmann, David Anderson, Rich Murphy, Christine Abunassar, and of course the team at Packt Publishing, Sarah, Joanna, Vishal, and Kedar. This has been AWESOME!

About the Reviewers

Eleanor Mante is an E-Learning Development Manager for one of the UK's largest newspaper publishers. She has been involved in IT and training in Canada and the UK for over 10 years.

As a Project Manager, E-Learning Designer, Microsoft Certified Trainer, and CIW Associate, Eleanor has worked with colleges, universities, and businesses to help them design and implement solutions.

She has worked with the following employers:

- Royal Bank of Canada
- Human Resources Development Canada
- Medbuy Corporation, Canada
- Fanshawe College, Canada
- University of Liverpool, UK
- Trinity Mirror PLC, UK

> I'd like to thank my wonderful family, partner, and friends for all of their support and encouragement over the years.

Mary Pienzi is an accomplished E-learning Developer who has been developing courses for 12 years. She began developing courses using tools such as Toolbook and Authorware, and then gradually moved into using Flash development as a courseware solution. Realizing that corporations were moving toward rapid development, she learned Articulate Presenter and its companions Engage and Quizmaker.

www.PacktPub.com

Support files, eBooks, discount offers and more

You might want to visit www.PacktPub.com for support files and downloads related to your book.

Did you know that Packt offers eBook versions of every book published, with PDF and ePub files available? You can upgrade to the eBook version at www.PacktPub.com and as a print book customer, you are entitled to a discount on the eBook copy. Get in touch with us at service@packtpub.com for more details.

At www.PacktPub.com, you can also read a collection of free technical articles, sign up for a range of free newsletters and receive exclusive discounts and offers on Packt books and eBooks.

http://PacktLib.PacktPub.com

Do you need instant solutions to your IT questions? PacktLib is Packt's online digital book library. Here, you can access, read and search across Packt's entire library of books.

Why Subscribe?

- Fully searchable across every book published by Packt
- Copy and paste, print and bookmark content
- On demand and accessible via web browser

Free Access for Packt account holders

If you have an account with Packt at www.PacktPub.com, you can use this to access PacktLib today and view nine entirely free books. Simply use your login credentials for immediate access.

Table of Contents

Preface

Articulate Studio '09 is a powerful authoring tool built to help both the expert trainer and the novice developer to quickly create useful learning experiences. While they can all work together, Articulate Studio '09 is a suite that contains four pieces of software that may be used individually or together. Therefore, this book will contain sections that may be used non-sequentially.

This book is meant to provide technical guidance for building a basic or complex course using the suite. While you are not limited in the creativity you can use in your course, this book will only provide a basic foundation for helping to develop a solid, polished course. You may find many additional and advanced techniques by visiting the Heroes forum on Articulate's website.

What this book covers

Chapter 1, Getting Started with Articulate Suite, covers the basics of the suite, what its capabilities are, and how to begin conceptualizing a basic course.

Chapter 2, Create Your Course with Presenter, covers the basics of creating a simple course using Presenter by itself. It teaches the basics of inserting media elements and assets, as well as preparing basic animations and finally publishing a simple course.

Chapter 3, Preparing Your Player, covers the features, setup, and capabilities of the Articulate Presenter course player. It provides guidance on how to edit color schemes, player elements, and functionality.

Chapter 4, Creating Assessments and Courses with Quizmaker, covers the core concepts behind the creation of basic assessment questions using Quizmaker. It covers the editing of the Quizmaker player and its functionality, and provides basic guidance on assessment creation using basic instructional design principles.

Chapter 5, *Taking Your Quiz to the Next Level*, shows the user how to use Quizmaker as more than just a basic quizzing tool. This chapter will include concepts on creating a more useful slide in the slide view, basic branching, and scenario concepts, as well as information on how to use Quizmaker to create a standalone course.

Chapter 6, *Creating Interactive Content with Engage*, discusses quick ways of adding interactive content to your course with Engage.

Chapter 7, *Basic Video Editing with Video Encoder*, guides the user through the process of basic video editing and file encoding using this tool. The user will learn how to perform basic tweaks as well as customize the video size and performance for your course.

Chapter 8, *Combining All Three*, shows the user how to finally combine all the three major applications from the suite into one cohesive course. They will also learn how to customize properties and course functionality.

What you need for this book

In order to get the maximum from this book, it is best to have the recommended software and hardware available, as well as an understanding of some basic concepts. It is recommended to have the following.

Software

Following are the software requirements:

- A PC running a current Windows operating system—Microsoft Windows 2000 SP4 or later (32 bit or 64 bit), Windows Vista (32 bit or 64 bit), or Windows 7 (32 bit or 64 bit), or a Mac computer running a Windows OS through Boot Camp, Parallels, or VMWare Fusion
- .NET 2.0 or later installed
- Microsoft PowerPoint 2003, 2007, or 2010 (32 bit)
- Microsoft Word 2000, 2003, 2007, or 2010
- Adobe Flash Player 6.0.79 or higher

Hardware

Following are the hardware requirements:

- At least a 1-GHz processor
- 1 GB of RAM (memory)
- A minimum disk space of 100 MB
- A working sound card and microphone (for recording narration), and optionally a webcam

Concepts

Following are the basic concepts required for this book:

- ▸ A basic understanding of PowerPoint and basic Word processing
- ▸ How to navigate to the ribbon in MS Office applications

Who this book is for

The typical readers of this book would be involved in the authoring of training or presentations, and would have a basic understanding of Microsoft Office tools such as PowerPoint and Word.

Conventions

In this book, you will find a number of styles of text that distinguish between different kinds of information. Here are some examples of these styles, and an explanation of their meaning.

Code words in text are shown as follows: "They must be recorded in either the .wav or .mp3 format."

New terms and **important words** are shown in bold. Words that you see on the screen, in menus or dialog boxes for example, appear in the text like this: "To import these files, click on the **Import Audio** button in the **Narration** section of the **Articulate** ribbon."

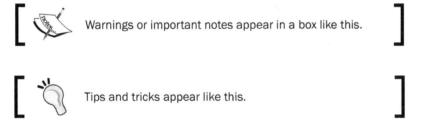

[Warnings or important notes appear in a box like this.]

[Tips and tricks appear like this.]

Reader feedback

Feedback from our readers is always welcome. Let us know what you think about this book—what you liked or may have disliked. Reader feedback is important for us to develop titles that you really get the most out of.

To send us general feedback, simply send an e-mail to feedback@packtpub.com, and mention the book title via the subject of your message.

If there is a topic that you have expertise in and you are interested in either writing or contributing to a book, see our author guide on www.packtpub.com/authors.

Customer support

Now that you are the proud owner of a Packt book, we have a number of things to help you to get the most from your purchase.

Errata

Although we have taken every care to ensure the accuracy of our content, mistakes do happen. If you find a mistake in one of our books—maybe a mistake in the text or the code—we would be grateful if you would report this to us. By doing so, you can save other readers from frustration and help us improve subsequent versions of this book. If you find any errata, please report them by visiting `http://www.packtpub.com/support`, selecting your book, clicking on the **errata submission form** link, and entering the details of your errata. Once your errata are verified, your submission will be accepted and the errata will be uploaded on our website, or added to any list of existing errata, under the Errata section of that title. Any existing errata can be viewed by selecting your title from `http://www.packtpub.com/support`.

Piracy

Piracy of copyright material on the Internet is an ongoing problem across all media. At Packt, we take the protection of our copyright and licenses very seriously. If you come across any illegal copies of our works, in any form, on the Internet, please provide us with the location address or website name immediately so that we can pursue a remedy.

Please contact us at `copyright@packtpub.com` with a link to the suspected pirated material.

We appreciate your help in protecting our authors, and our ability to bring you valuable content.

Questions

You can contact us at `questions@packtpub.com` if you are having a problem with any aspect of the book, and we will do our best to address it.

1
Getting Started with Articulate Suite

In this chapter we will cover:

- ▸ Launching Articulate Presenter
- ▸ Publishing a simple, slide-only course for a website
- ▸ Adding a background theme
- ▸ Modifying slide masters
- ▸ Adding a learning game to your course

Introduction

Congratulations! You've just bought and installed Articulate Studio '09, one of the most popular and easiest to use e-learning development tools available in today's market. Sure there are other tools, but among corporate users, Articulate is a popular choice. Why is this? Because their organizations have already been working on the Microsoft Office platform and they are used to working in Microsoft PowerPoint. As a matter of fact, many of them have huge libraries of training materials that they have already developed for use in PowerPoint. When making the decision to transition to an e-learning platform, their familiarity with PowerPoint makes the transition easy.

Articulate Studio is a complete suite that comes with four applications, namely Presenter, Engage, Quizmaker, and Video Encoder. These four applications work together, and in some cases individually, to help you produce a Flash-based, e-learning course with minimal programming expertise.

We're going to start out by focusing on Articulate Presenter. This application is not a standalone application like the others in the suite; instead it is a PowerPoint plugin. In other words, you need to have Microsoft PowerPoint installed on your computer in order to use Articulate Presenter.

Additionally, you need to be aware that Articulate Studio is a Windows-only application. It will not work with the Mac OSX versions of Microsoft Office. However, if you are on a Mac-based system, you may install Windows through the use of programs such as boot camp (which comes preinstalled in Mac OSX) or emulation software such as Parallels and VMWare Fusion.

Launching Articulate Presenter

Once you have Articulate installed on your computer, you can run any of the four programs that are part of the Articulate suite. Articulate Presenter functions as a plugin for Microsoft PowerPoint. Although the four programs are standalone applications, they are intended to work together. Articulate Presenter is the main program while Engage, Quizmaker, and Video Encoder can produce standalone, finished products.

How to do it...

When the Articulate suite is installed on your computer, it should provide you with desktop icons for all four of the programs in the Suite. This is the easiest way to access any of the programs in the Suite:

1. If you have installed the Articulate Studio Suite, you should have an icon for Articulate Presenter on your computer's desktop. Double-click on the icon and a dialog box should appear.

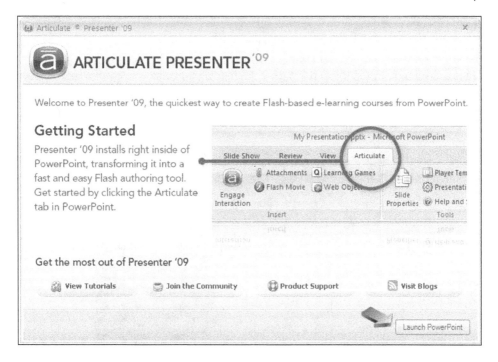

This dialog box gives you basic information about the application and how it should appear in your PowerPoint application.

 On the launch screen there are a series of buttons for **View Tutorials**, **Join the Community**, **Product Support**, and **Visit Blogs**. These buttons take you to recourses that are located on Articulate's website.

2. Note that at the bottom right-hand side of the dialog box it now says **Launch PowerPoint**. Clicking on this button will open PowerPoint with the Articulate plugin.

3. Once you have opened up PowerPoint, check that the **Articulate** tab has been included on the ribbon.

How it works...

If you need to perform this recovery feature, you will need to make sure to have administrator privileges on your computer. If you don't have such privileges, ask your system administrator for assistance.

There's more...

There is also another way to access Articulate Presenter. Since Presenter is a plugin of PowerPoint, it opens whenever PowerPoint is opened.

The other method of launching Articulate Presenter is simply by going to **Start | Programs | Microsoft Office** on your computer's desktop and double-clicking on the Microsoft PowerPoint application. Launching it in this way actually cuts out a step for those concerned about efficiency.

Recovering from startup errors

While Articulate Presenter is a stable application that works well, it is still a PowerPoint plugin. So like any software, from time to time, there's the possibility of errors happening. When these happen, don't be too alarmed. There are ways of recovering from most of the things that can happen:

1. If the **Articulate** tab is not there, you can get it back. If you are using PowerPoint 2010, start by clicking on **File** and then **Options**. If you are using PowerPoint 2007, start by clicking on the **Office** button, and then click on the PowerPoint **Options** button at the bottom of the menu.

2. A PowerPoint **Options** dialog box will appear; click on **Add-Ins**.

3. At the bottom of the dialog box, where the **Manage** select box is, select **COM Add-Ins**.

4. Click on the **Go...** button.

5. A **COM Add-Ins** dialog box will appear. Look for a line that says **Articulate Presenter Ribbon** and make sure it is checked. If not, check it; then click on **OK**.

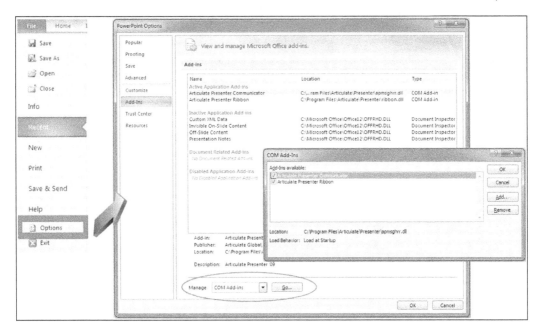

Once these steps are completed, the Articulate tab should appear in PowerPoint.

Publishing a simple, slide-only course for a website

Articulate handles presentations differently from PowerPoint, creating a Flash animation video (a .swf file) out of it. This means that Articulate has to publish the presentation and not just save it as PowerPoint does. The published presentation consists of two parts, the presentation itself and the player. The player folder is the skin with the controls and other information about the presentation. In addition to controlling the slides of the course, it also allows access to other files if they have been added to the course.

When finished, each slide becomes its own Flash file. This allows for fast downloading by users who are accessing the course or presentation via the Internet. Additional content, such as a glossary, would be a separate Flash file accessible through the player.

Getting ready

Any presentation will consist of a number of slides. These slides may contain any of the text, graphics, and objects that PowerPoint can produce, along with other content that is created in Articulate Presenter or the other programs contained in the Articulate suite. We will be showing you how to add this material throughout this course.

In order to walk through the process of publishing a presentation, we're going to need a presentation that we can use. You can either open an existing PowerPoint presentation that you have on your computer or create a simple one. I've created a simple, three-slide presentation about the nursery rhyme "Mary Had a Little Lamb".

How to do it...

Once you have your presentation, there are two parts to accomplishing this recipe. The first one consists of creating the player template. Once we have created the template, we'll use that template to publish our simple course.

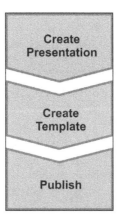

As you can see from this flow diagram, the process is a logical one. Typically, one starts by creating the presentation before creating or choosing the template. In this way, the template can be made to match the needs of the presentation.

Creating the template

1. The first thing we're going to need is a player template. This will tell Articulate how to set up the player when the presentation is published. Click on the **Player Templates** button in the **Tools** section of the **Articulate** ribbon.

2. The **Player Templates** dialog box will open. As we've already seen in other Articulate dialog boxes, this one also has a set of tabs along the left-hand side. It should open with the **Layout** tab highlighted; if not, select it.

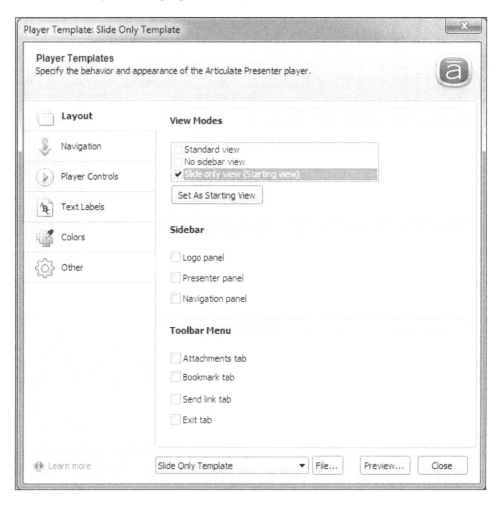

3. The only change we want to make here at this time is in the **View Modes**. You will probably find all three tick boxes checked on the upper part of the center pane. Deselect the **Standard view** and **No sidebar view**, leaving only the **Slide only view (Starting view)** tick box checked.

4. We're now going to save these settings as a new player template. To do so, go to the drop-down list at the bottom of the dialog box. It will say **Corporate Communications**. Since we want this to be a new template, we're going to click on the button to the right of it that says **File...**, and select **Save As...** from the menu. A small dialog box opens for us to type in the new template's name. Let's call this one **Slide Only Template**.

Publishing the Course

1. Now that we have our template set up, we can go on to publish the presentation. Close the **Player Templates** dialog box and select the **Publish** button from the **Articulate** ribbon.

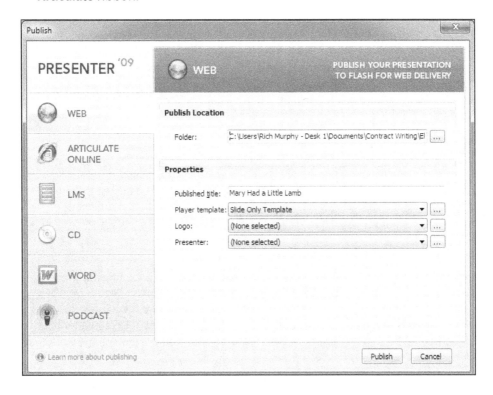

2. To do this, we'll need to be on the **Web** tab. The first thing we need to do is to provide the **Publish Location**. If you don't want to use the default location shown in the **Folder** area, click on the button to the right-hand side of the location (arrow 1 in the screenshot) and select the folder you would like to place the published presentation in. You can also type the location directly into the provided area (arrow 2 in the screenshot).

3. Dropping a little further down in the dialog box, we find an area called **Properties**. We'll need to give our presentation a name in the **Published title** area (arrow 3 on the screenshot). This is the name that will appear in the presentation window header when the presentation is published. Therefore, you want to use a proper name for the presentation. Finally we need to tell the program what template to use. We're going to select **Slide Only Template** (the template we just created) from the drop-down list.

4. We are now ready to publish our presentation. All we have to do is click on the **Publish** button in the dialog box and the program will do the rest.

5. Depending on the length of your presentation, publishing may take several minutes. To make this process run as fast as possible and reduce the chance of errors, it is recommended to not use your computer for other operations while Articulate is creating your Flash presentation. If you use copy and paste, what you have copied will show up in your presentation.

How it works...

As you can see from the tabs in the **Publish** dialog box, Articulate can publish your finished Flash presentation in a number of ways. The first tab, the one we used, creates the necessary files for publishing to the Web. You can also use this option for publishing on your computer for local use.

> Before you start publishing presentations, it's important to realize that not everything that PowerPoint does is supported by Articulate; specifically, the slide transitions aren't supported. So if you're accustomed to using transitions between your slides, you'll have to forgo that in Articulate Presenter. Likewise, not all animations from PowerPoint are supported. Later we'll show you which ones are.

Once you start working in Articulate Presenter, it creates a second file for your presentation. So instead of only having a `.pptx` file from PowerPoint, you will also have a `.ppta` file. The name will be the same, and only the file extension will be different. If you need to move your presentation to another folder on your computer or put it on removable media for it to work on another computer, be sure to copy both the files, otherwise you will lose all the work that you did in Articulate.

The Flash presentations that Articulate creates are noneditable Flash files. This provides a great advantage over standard PowerPoint files, which can be modified by the end user. In training and sales presentation situations, where the user is viewing the presentation on their own, there is no possibility of the viewer accidentally or intentionally making changes to the file.

Once Articulate has finished publishing your Flash presentation, it will notify you by displaying the **Publish Successful** dialog box. This provides you with a number of options, including the ability to view your presentation, upload it to the Web via FTP, or compress it in a ZIP file.

If you open the folder that contains your presentation, you will see that it consists of a number of files. The folder will be titled with the name of the presentation, and it will contain two folders (titled `data` and `player`) and a `player.HTML` file. The player file is the one that you click to play the presentation. It will open in whatever program the user has selected as your default for Flash files, probably their default web browser.

You can rename this file as desired. However, don't rename the folders. If you need to copy, move, or upload your presentation, be sure to move the entire folder, including the subfolders and the player file. Otherwise, your flash presentation will not work.

Adding a background theme

Artistic design is an important part of creating a presentation. You want people's eyes to be attracted to your presentation, and even more importantly, you want it to hold their attention. That's pretty much impossible to do if your presentation isn't attractive.

You also want your presentation to provide some identity with the subject matter and/or your company's brand. Whether designing a presentation for a training session, corporate proposal, or sales, you need to be able to tie the whole thing together, providing visual continuity so that the viewer understands that it is all part of one continuous theme.

At this point, the theme we are creating only deals with the presentation and not the skin. That will be done at another time. For the best possible results, you want your presentation theme and your skin theme to go together. It is helpful to keep your skin theme colors in mind while creating your presentation theme.

There are actually several ingredients in creating this visual theme, such as the background image, the placement of objects on the slides, and the text size, style, and color. For this reason, it is very useful to start the creation of your presentation by applying a theme to the slides in the presentation. Microsoft PowerPoint has this capability built-in along with a number of themes that are available for its use.

How to do it...

Themes are created using PowerPoint's capability rather than Articulate's. However, the skin theme is created in Articulate:

1. To access these themes, you need to click on the **Design** tab at the top of the PowerPoint screen. Your ribbon should change to show the following screenshot:

2. Selecting from PowerPoint's installed themes only requires clicking on the theme's thumbnail on the ribbon.

 Please note that not all the themes are visible at once. Clicking on the scroll bar to the right-hand side of the shown themes allows you to scroll through all the themes you have installed on your system. The arrow with the line at the bottom of the scroll bar is for opening the drop-down that shows all the installed themes at once.

How it works...

Selecting a theme for a presentation gives us the following:

- ▸ Background options
- ▸ Text styles
- ▸ Color pallets

There's more...

The themes themselves are fully customizable. There are three buttons located to the right-hand side of the shown themes, which provide for the customization of the colors, fonts, and effects in the theme.

Changing theme colors

By clicking on the **Colors** button in the **Themes** section of the ribbon, a drop-down appears that allows the selection of the existing color themes. This may be divided into two separate areas depending upon the selected theme, the upper section showing the color themes that are available for that particular theme, and the lower section listing all of the color themes that are built-in to Microsoft Office.

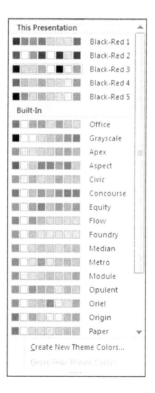

For most themes, selecting a color theme doesn't affect the background color; it affects the text and bullet point colors. However, there are a few themes that change to match the color scheme selected. You'll have to play with the theme you are using to see what changes it allows you to make. If none of the included color themes satisfy your need, you can modify them by selecting **Create New Theme Colors...** from the bottom of the drop-down list. This opens a dialog box for creating a new color theme.

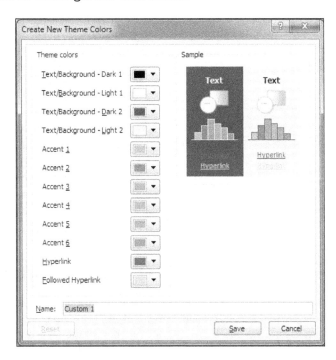

By selecting one of the existing color themes, you can use it as your starting point for creating your new color theme. The theme shown in the screenshot of the dialog box is the "Text" theme. Each type of **Text**, **Accent**, and **Hyperlink** theme can be individually changed. Your new color theme can then be saved under whatever name you choose.

To change the background color, one would need to select **Background Styles** in the **Background** section of the ribbon. Since in many cases the backgrounds are pictures, you are somewhat limited to the amount of color change that you can make. However, there are some themes that are not images, but rather are designs that are appropriate for being used as the background. In these cases, you can change colors, add a texture, or change from a solid fill to a gradient. This varies from theme to theme, depending upon what is built in to that theme.

Changing theme fonts

Selecting **Fonts** from the **Themes** section on the ribbon allows you to select any of the standard Microsoft Office font style sets. These are the same font style sets that are used in Microsoft Word and other office applications.

Just as with the color themes, the font themes are fully customizable. Selecting **Create New Theme Fonts...** at the bottom of the **Fonts** drop-down opens a dialog box for selecting the heading and body fonts that you want to use in your theme. These can then be saved as a new font theme.

The reason that you can only select the heading and body fonts rather than select a variety of different fonts is that, artistically speaking, it is not recommended to use more than two fonts in a document. You still have the availability to individually change the font of a specific word, line, or page of text if you so desire, but that would not be a part of the font theme.

Changing theme effects

The final area of customization available for your theme is the effects, selectable by clicking on the **Effects** button in the **Themes** section of the ribbon. The **Effects** drop-down provides a selection of the different effects that can be used in the theme. These effects are automatically applied to buttons and other objects in the presentation as a part of the theme.

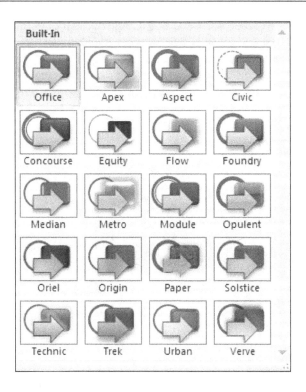

Saving your changed theme

Once you make changes to a theme, you can save that modified theme under a new name. This would be especially useful if you needed to create a series of presentations and wanted to maintain branding throughout the series.

To save your new theme, open the **Themes** dropbox by clicking on the button at the bottom of the scroll bar to the right-hand side of the theme thumbnails. At the bottom of the dropbox it will say **Save Current Theme....** Clicking on this opens the standard, Windows **Save As...** dialog box, which will be open to the themes folder on your computer.

Adding a theme from Microsoft.com or third-party websites

Although Microsoft PowerPoint comes with a number of themes preinstalled, it may not have the theme that you want for the presentation you are trying to produce. Never fear, that has already been considered, and the ability to add themes has been built right into PowerPoint.

You can find themes on Microsoft's website and a large number of third-party websites who produce them both for free and for sale. Both of these sources can be used and added to your personal copy of PowerPoint.

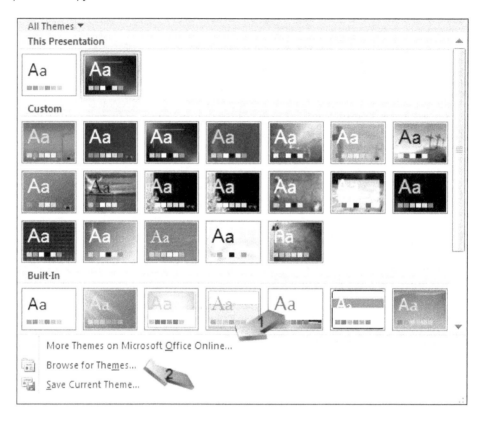

To search for and add themes from Microsoft, click on the button at the bottom of the scroll bar to the right-hand side of the themes thumbnails to open the themes drop-down list. On the bottom of this drop-down, you will see the words **More Themes on Microsoft Office Online...**. Clicking on that legend will take you to the themes page on the Microsoft website.

The web page will show you a variety of themes for all of the Microsoft Office products. Since we are working in PowerPoint, you will want to select the PowerPoint themes by using the button on the left-hand side of the screen.

Selecting a theme allows you to download it to your computer. This is essentially the same procedure you would use to select and download a theme from a third-party website. While the details will vary with the website, the idea is the same.

Themes consist of several files, so they are downloaded as a `.zip` file. You will need to unzip the file to a location on your hard drive in order to input it into a PowerPoint or Articulate presentation. Once the theme is downloaded and unzipped, you will need to find the theme, bring it into PowerPoint, and click on the legend **Browse for Themes...** on the themes drop-down list. This will open a standard Windows dialog box, allowing you to search for and select the theme and follow the prompts to install the new theme. It will show up immediately in PowerPoint without restarting.

Modifying slide masters

What we talked about in the last recipe is how a theme allows us to have consistent background, colors, and fonts. Those are all part of the theme. However, one of the great tools that PowerPoint provides that is extremely useful to us in creating Articulate presentations is the ability to create slide masters. These slide masters are the part of the template that controls what objects show up on each page. If we want to have a title on each page, as is common in PowerPoint presentations, placing a textbox for it on the slide master ensures that it will be located in the same place and be the same size on each slide.

Getting ready

You can find the button for the slide masters by clicking on the **View** tab. The **Slide Master** button appears on the **Presentation Views** section of the ribbon.

When the slide master appears, it will show the first slide master in the set as in the main editable part of the screen. To the left-hand side of the pane, where the thumbnails of the slides are normally shown, you will see the thumbnails of all the slide masters in the set, one for every layout option (there are usually 10). At the same time, the **Slide Master** tab will appear, allowing access to the Slide Master ribbon.

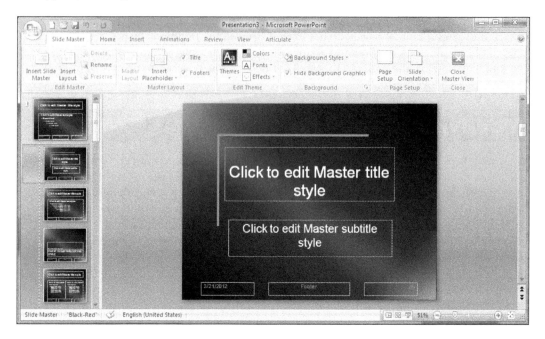

To create a totally new theme, you would start by clicking the **Insert Slide Master** button on the ribbon. This will insert a blank master set, which includes all the layouts that are in the current set. If you do this and then delete the existing master, you will have an entire new set of slide masters.

How to do it...

Creating a slide master consists of placing the things on the master that you want to have show up in all your slides. This can be done in one of two ways so that they are all on all the slides regardless of the type, or so that they are only on one type of slide layout.

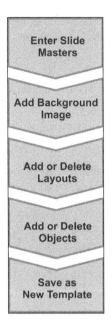

A complete slide master not only deals with the background and objects that you want to show on all the slides, but also with all the layout options for the slides. Don't forget to make the necessary modifications to all the different layouts:

1. The first thing you want to do on your master is to add an image in the background. This is done in the same way as inserting an image in a regular slide, using the **Picture** button on the **Insert** ribbon.

This image should be 720 x 540 pixels in size. If you download background images from the Internet, they will typically be this size. If you are using your own image, you may need to resize it or crop it to these dimensions. When you insert the image, it may not show up as filling the entire page. This would indicate that the image is not 720 x 540 pixels.

Although the background image is covering the other elements in the master, it will not be covering them in the normal work view. However, if you need to work with those elements, changing them in some way, you will want to arrange the background image at the back, as we discussed in the *How it Works...* section in the *Launching Articulate Presenter* recipe.

2. To delete a layout from the set, select its thumbnail from the list in the left-hand side panel of the PowerPoint screen. Click on the **Delete** button on the **Slide Master** ribbon or right-click on the thumbnail and select **Delete Layout** from the context-sensitive menu.

3. You can also add another layout to the master set by clicking on the **Insert Layout** button on the ribbon. This allows you to create your own layout, which is totally different from the standard layouts included in PowerPoint.

 There are two categories of objects that can be added to the master, namely regular objects and object placeholders. Regular objects are anything that you want showing up on all the slides. Placeholders are used for inserting information, such as pictures, text, or charts later.

4. Regular objects are placed on the master just as they are onto individual slides. Select the object that you want to insert from the **Insert ribbon** and place it on the master slide.

5. To make these same objects show up in the same place on the title slide, as on the other slides, place them on the master, then copy them, select the Master Slide, and paste them.

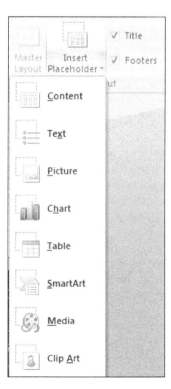

6. Clicking on the arrow next to the **Insert Placeholder** legend of the **Insert Placeholder** button on the **Slide Master** ribbon opens the drop-down, which allows you to select what type of placeholder you want to place on the master. Do not use **Media** placeholders on your slide masters as media will be inserted in Articulate.

7. Once you select the type of the placeholder you wish to put on your slide master, you must place it on the slide. To do so, go to the corner of the area where you want the placeholder, click-and-hold your left mouse button, and drag it to the opposite corner, releasing the button there. This will create the placeholder.

 Placeholders are the dotted line boxes that you see already in place on the slide masters. They allow you to insert the content in a consistent manner across all the slides of your presentation. As you can see by looking at the master slide set, PowerPoint makes extensive use of placeholders. This is an important part of maintaining visual continuity throughout your presentation.

How it works...

Looking at the thumbnails on the left-hand side pane of the PowerPoint window, you can see that the top one is larger, with the rest of the thumbnails connected to it as in a branched directory tree. That's because the first one is the master while the others are the various layouts that exist for that master. Any changes you make to the master, such as adding an image, will show up in all the layouts. Changes made to the individual layouts will only show up in that particular layout.

The exception to this rule is when you are dealing with the title slide. Changes made to the set do not affect the title slide, as many people have different title slides, but they are similar to the other layouts in the set.

There's more...

There is an alternative way of accessing the various changes that we've made in this recipe, and that is to use the **Edit Theme** that is a part of the **Slide Master** ribbon. This provides the exact same changes to the theme as we saw in the **Design** ribbon.

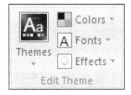

Turning on Date, Slide number, and Footer placeholders

Along the bottom of every slide master are the placeholders for the date, slide number, and footer. Although these placeholders exist, they are normally hidden. To use them in your presentation, they need to be turned on. To do this, exit the slide master view by clicking on the **Close Master View** button on the **Slide Master** ribbon.

In the **Insert** ribbon, click on the **Header & Footer** button to open the **Header and Footer** dialog box. You can click on the radio buttons you desire for turning on the **Date and time**, **Slide number**, and **Footer** object placeholders. The **Footer** allows you a place to insert the text you want on the footer. **Date and time** allows you to choose between having the date automatically update to the current date or the date and time of the presentation, or to having a fixed date showing the date of your choice, such as the release date for the presentation.

Hyperlinks and the slide master

You can also add a hyperlink for any object on the slide master. This is done in the same way as in PowerPoint. The same hyperlink will show up and function on all the pages of the presentation. This would be especially useful for branching your presentation to various subjects or chapters.

You can also place an object on your slide master, which will be hyperlinked to different places on each slide. You can do this by placing the object on the slide master but creating the hyperlink on each slide.

Creating transparent hyperlinks

Let's say that you are creating a sales presentation demonstrating the benefits of a particular piece of technology. You want to make your presentation usable by both the general public and by engineers who will want to see the technical specifications for each feature. You can create your master slide with a series of buttons in the corner, essentially creating a button bar. Then you can create your presentation with each slide, showing a different feature for each piece of equipment.

The **Home** and **Directory** buttons can be hyperlinked directly on the slide master as they will be the same for all the slides. The **Specs** hyperlink will be different on each slide, so it cannot be hyperlinked on the master slide. Its hyperlinks will have to be done on each individual slide. But by putting the graphic button object on the master, we can ensure that it is always in the same place.

On the individual slides, another object will need to be placed over the **Specs.** button, in this case, a transparent rectangle. That object can then be made transparent by giving it no fill and no outline on the **Format** tab. This transparent object can then be hyperlinked just like any other object. That will allow the engineers to go to the detailed specs for that particular feature.

Adding a learning game to your course

Articulate Quizmaker gives you the capability of creating extensive quizzes and other interactive activities; however, there is also a built-in capacity for creating interactive learning games that is a part of Articulate Presenter. This capability gives you the ability of creating three different learning games right in your Articulate presentation. Having this capability allows you to make the lesson more interactive and ask questions to the learner.

Putting a learning game into your presentation can do a lot to help engage the learners in the training being provided. This will help them grasp the material that is being presented better and retain it longer.

How to do it...

The learning games provided directly in Articulate Presenter are much simpler than those that can be created in Quizmaker. However, when something quick and simple is needed, this is much easier than creating a quiz and importing it into a presentation.

The learning games are accessed off the **Articulate** ribbon in PowerPoint by clicking on the **Learning Games** button:

1. Clicking on the button opens a dialog box that will allow you to select between adding a new learning game and editing an existing one. Since we have not yet added a learning game to our presentation, the edit option will be grayed out, leaving our only option to **Add a new learning game slide**.

It should be noted that any time that you add a learning game, it will be added to your presentation as a new slide immediately following the currently selected slide. Of course, like any other slide in a PowerPoint presentation, it can be moved through the order of the presentation by clicking and moving its thumbnail to the left-hand side pane of the work area.

There are three types of learning games that you can choose for your presentation, namely **Choices**, **Word Quiz**, and **Sequence**. We're going to do the **Choices** type. The others are done in a very similar manner.

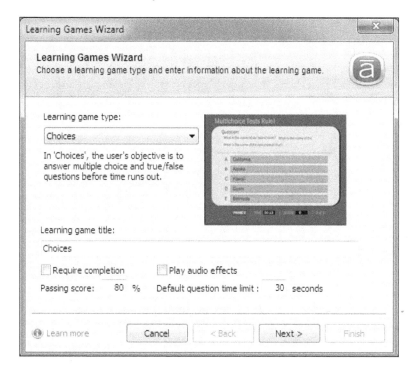

2. The **Learning Games Wizard** dialog will show **Choices** as the default **Learning game type**.

3. Select the **Require completion** checkbox in the lower part of the dialog box. This will ensure that the viewer must complete the game before continuing on to the next part of the presentation.

4. In the **Passing score** textbox, input 70 for a required passing grade of 70 percent to move on to the rest of the presentation.

5. Click on the **Next** button at the bottom of the wizard's dialog box. Here you can type in any custom message to be displayed before the game starts. Type in `Answer the questions about Mary's Lamb` in the text area. Be sure to check the checkbox so that the message will be displayed.

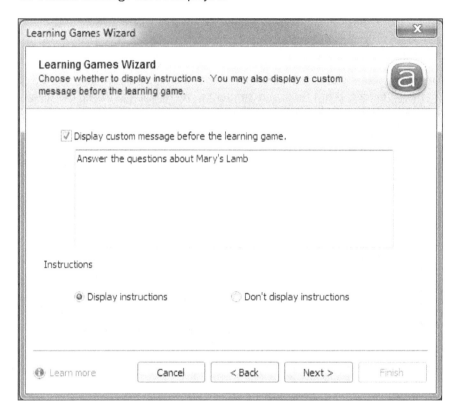

6. In the **Instructions** section select **Display instructions**. If you do not wish to provide instructions to the user, click on **Don't display instructions**.

7. Click on the **Next** button to insert the questions. Click on the **Add** button to type in a new question. Add the questions shown in the screenshot.

8. The questions will appear in a list, allowing you to reorder them as you choose. To reorder them, use the buttons outlined in red in the following screenshot:

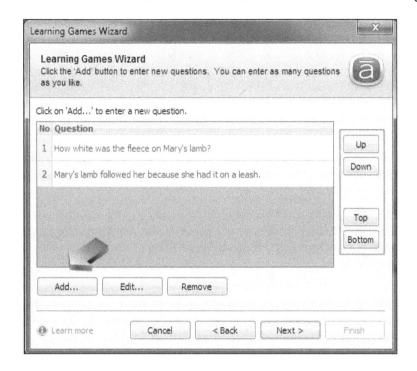

 At this point, the dialog box is going to be context specific for the type of learning game you are creating. Regardless of which type of learning game you are creating, you will be adding one question and its answers in the same dialog box. You can continue adding as many questions as you like to the game. However, for each game, you'll need to supply the correct answer. In the case of multiple choice, you'll need to supply the correct answer and as many as four false answers.

9. Once you have finished inserting and checking your questions and answers, click on the **Next** button to create any custom feedback for the learner.

10. Once the feedback is inserted, click on the **Next** button to create the learning game.

11. Articulate will add a placeholder slide in the order of the slide thumbnails on the left-hand side pane of your PowerPoint screen. You will not be able to see the learning game unless you preview or publish it. To preview the game, click on the **Preview** button in the **Publish** section of the **Articulate** ribbon.

12. It will take the program a moment to render your game in a functioning, viewable version. This will show you exactly how it will look when you view it in the final presentation. It will also allow you to test the game, making sure that the questions and answers function correctly and that you are satisfied with how it looks.

How it works...

The learning games are added to the presentation via a wizard, which creates the game from the information you fill in. The **Learning Game Wizard**, which opens once you click on the **OK** button of the previous dialog box, walks you through the process of creating the game.

Although you can fully customize the content of your learning game, you can't customize the appearance of it. Within Articulate Presenter, you are limited to the default game style. If you would like to be able to further customize your game, create it in Articulate Quizmaker. We will discuss how to do this in *Chapter 3, Preparing Your Player*.

One last detail about your learning game. Now that you've created a learning game in your presentation, when you click on the **Learning Games** button on the ribbon, you now have the option of editing previously created learning games. To do this, click on the **Edit an existing learning game slide** radio button, and then use the drop-down menu to select from the various learning games that you have in your presentation.

To preview the learning game, click on the **Preview** tab in the **Articulate** ribbon and you will see the following screenshot:

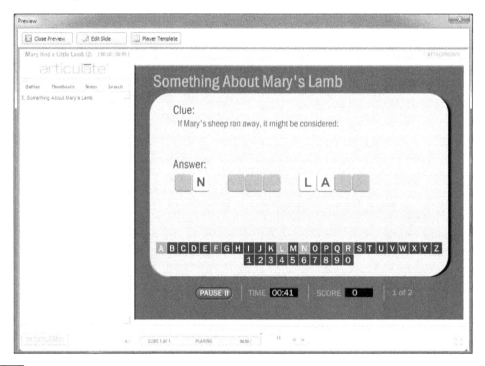

There's more...

There are three types of learning games included in Articulate, as follows:

- ▸ **Choices**: This creates a multiple choice or true/false quiz
- ▸ **Word Quiz**: This creates a "Hangman" or "Wheel of Fortune" type of game
- ▸ **Sequence**: This is where the learner puts things in order

The **Choices** game allows you to select between **Multiple choice** and **True/False**. In both cases, you enter the question and your answers. You must also tell the wizard which answer is the correct one.

The **Word Quiz** game allows you to enter only the question and the answer. The answer will be what they are trying to guess the letters for.

The **Sequence** game allows you to enter up to seven items, which the learner must put in order. You enter them in the correct order and the program randomizes them for you.

The following screenshot is for adding **Multiple choice** questions to the **Choices** learning game. Please note that towards the bottom you can select the amount of time given to the learner to select the correct answer. This option exists with all the games, for all types of questions. The default will be whatever you selected for the game back in the first step of the **Learning Game Wizard** dialog box. However, you can customize the length of the time that will be allowed for each question.

You can select the type of game you want from the **learning game type** drop-down menu on the **Learning Games Wizard** dialog box. Selecting a game type changes the thumbnail in the dialog box, providing visual recognition of the type of game you have selected. You can also input the name for your game in the area **Learning game title**. In the lower part of the dialog box, there are selections available for the customization of the gameplay:

- ▶ **Require completion**: Selecting this radio button prevents the learner from moving on until they have successfully completed the learning game.
- ▶ **Play audio effects**: Selecting this radio button plays built-in sound effects for the game. The sound effects are built into the program and cannot be changed.
- ▶ **Passing score**: The default for this is **80%**, but it can be changed to any figure you want.
- ▶ **Default question time limit**: The default for this is **30** seconds for the **Choices** game and **60** seconds for the other types. However, it can be changed to any time you want.

2
Create Your Course with Presenter

In this chapter we will cover:

- ▶ Animating images and objects
- ▶ Adding audio narration to your slides
- ▶ Editing audio
- ▶ Adding background music to your presentation
- ▶ Syncing the animations with narrations
- ▶ Adding video to your course
- ▶ Adding video from the Web
- ▶ Highlighting specific slide information

Introduction

In the first chapter, we briefly explored how to put a presentation together and publish it; however, Articulate Presenter has much more capability than what we've already explored. So now we're going to start exploring what you can really do with Articulate Presenter.

Please keep in mind that we will be using the capability of PowerPoint, just as we did in the last chapter. However, we are not going to use PowerPoint for inserting any media files into the presentation; instead, we'll insert them via Articulate. In this chapter you'll learn how to do this.

Everything you will need to access for creating your final Articulate Flash video presentation is on the **Articulate** ribbon in PowerPoint. Here you will find the necessary tools for creating the player skin, inserting media into the presentation, and establishing your presentation's defaults. You will also be telling the presentation how to play, what to allow the viewer or learner to do, and creating any narration to go with the Flash video presentation.

We will be working with buttons in all the sections of the **Articulate** ribbon in PowerPoint. While the steps we will be going through may seem a bit complex, fear not; Articulate gives us the capability to save the settings we create as templates for future presentations. So let's start by understanding how to set up a player template.

Animating images and objects

Animating your objects is done on the Animations ribbon. Please note that this ribbon is different on PowerPoint 2010 than it is on PowerPoint 2007. Just about everything you do will be the same, however the locations and names of some things may be different. For the purpose of this book, we're going to look at PowerPoint 2010, but we will tell you about the differences.

Getting ready

To start we'll need a slide with a couple of objects on it. You can copy a slide from an existing presentation, putting it into a new presentation to experiment with. I'm going to use the first slide from our "Mary Had a Little Lamb" presentation. So that we can do anything we want to with this slide, I'm going to add a few buttons and an arrow to it, giving us some more objects to work with.

When animating objects, it can be extremely useful to group them. This causes the animation to act on the group of objects as if they are one object. To group two or more objects, select them together, then right-click on one of the objects. Click on the **Group** button; it will open another fly-out menu, then click on **Group**.

How to do it...

Animations can only be done to already existing objects. Often, it is easiest to place all the objects on the slide before beginning the animations. That makes it easier to see how the animations will react with one another. For animating images and objects, perform the following steps:

1. Open up the **Selections** pane by clicking on the **Selection Pane** button in the **Arrange** section of the **Format** ribbon. This will help you keep track of the various objects on the slide and their order of layering.

2. To rename the objects, click on the name in the **Selections** pane and type in a new name. The small button to the right-hand side of each object's name is for making the object visible or invisible.

3. Open the **Animation** pane in the **Animations** ribbon. For PowerPoint 2010, click on the **Animation Pane** button in the **Advanced Animation** section of the ribbon. For PowerPoint 2007, click on the **Custom Animation** button in the **Animations** section of the **Animations** ribbon.

4. Adding an animation to a particular object consists of selecting the object and then selecting the animation for it. On the 2010 ribbon, you can add an animation either by clicking on the animation's icon in the center part of the ribbon, or by clicking on the **Add Animation** button in the **Advanced Animations** section of the ribbon. Clicking on this button opens the **Animation** drop-down menu, as shown in the following screenshot:

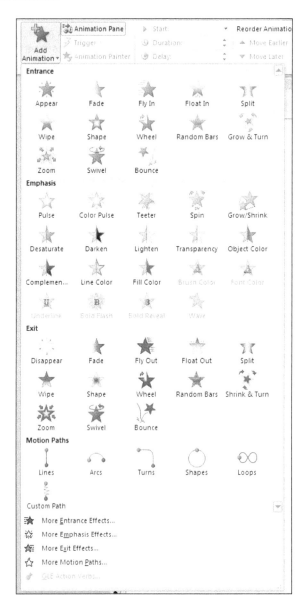

5. Select the animation you want by clicking on it.

How it works...

When you first open the **Selection** pane, the objects will all appear with names such as **Rounded Rectangle 12**, **TextBox 13**, and **Picture 14**. This numbering will be sequential in the order that the objects have been added to that slide. The order in which the objects appear in the pane is the order in which they are layered in the slide. The top object that is listed is the top one in the order. To change the order, right-click on the object and select **Bring to Top** or **Send to Bottom** on the context-sensitive menu.

PowerPoint works like a desktop publishing program in the same way that it handles the ordering and layering of the objects. If you were doing the design that you are doing in PowerPoint on paper, gluing blocks of text, pictures, and other objects to the paper would have caused some of them to overlap others. This is the concept of "layering". Every object that you put on a slide is layered even if none of them overlap each other. When they do overlap each other, the objects that were added later overlap the earlier ones. This can be changed by changing the object order, using **Bring to Top**, **Send Forward**, **Send Backward**, and **Send to Bottom** in the context-sensitive menu.

The **Animation** dropbox itself shows the most popular animations and is divided into four, color-coded sections for the type of animation that is to be added, as follows:

- The **Entrance** animations are green
- The **Emphasis** animations are yellow or gray
- The **Exit** animations are red
- The **Motion Paths** animations are multicolored

In addition, there are links at the bottom of the dialog box to access more animations than the ones shown in the dropbox. Selecting an animation automatically adds it to the **Animations** pane, so that you can see it.

The animations you have added will be listed in the **Animations** pane in the order in which they run. There will be an icon of a mouse as well, to show that the animation is intended to run with the click of a mouse. The numbers to the left-hand side of the animation tell you what order they are in. If an animation does not have a number to its left-hand side, it is set to run with the previous one. If it has a clock face to the left-hand side, it is intended to run after the previous animation, as shown in the following screenshot:

Even though we're setting the animations to start with a mouse click, that won't actually be happening in the Flash video. Later we'll be sequencing the animations, syncing them with the narration. We will need them to be activated by a mouse click in order to do this.

There's more...

There are a number of different changes you can make to how your animations are run.

Animation timing

Articulate offers the capability to precisely time your animations, which is much easier than what PowerPoint offers. This makes it easier to match the timing of the animations with the narration. Perform the following steps:

1. By right-clicking on any of the animations, you can access a context-sensitive menu, which allows you to select the animations to run on a mouse click, concurrent with the previous animation or after the previous animation. This can be done using options such as **Start On Click**, **Start With Previous**, and **Start After Previous**, as shown in the following screenshot:

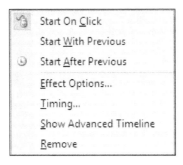

2. For some animations you can change other settings, such as the direction that the object enters the slide from. This is done by clicking on **Effect Options...** in the context-sensitive menu.

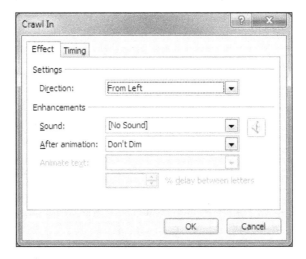

3. When the dialog box opens, you can set **Direction** or any other setting particular to that animation in the upper part of the dialog box.

4. You can add sound effects to the animation using the **Sound** drop-down menu in the lower part of the dialog box.

5. Clicking on **Timing** in the context-sensitive menu opens a dialog box that allows you to change the speed with which the animations run, as shown in the following screenshot:

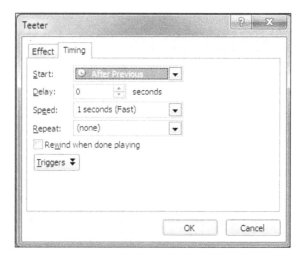

6. There are five settings available in the **Speed** drop-down menu, from very slow to very fast. As you can see from the preceding screenshot, the program tells you how long the animation will run for at each speed.

7. Using the **Repeat** drop-down menu, you can set the animation to repeat itself a set number of times until the slide ends or until the next mouse click.

8. The context-sensitive menu also allows you to open an advanced timeline by clicking on **Show Advanced Timeline**, which will allow you to further fine-tune your animation and its timing, including adding a delay between it and the previous animation. The timeline view allows you to see how the overlap and running of your animations will come out in terms of seconds.

> You never want to have the first animation in the slide run automatically; you only want to have it run on the mouse click. Setting it to **Start With Previous** or **Start After Previous** is not compatible with Flash animation.

Multiple animations

Multiple animations can be used for a single object. You can bring the item in with an entrance animation, have a second animation performed on it for emphasis, and then have it exit with an exit animation. These can either be one after the other, or with other things happening in between them.

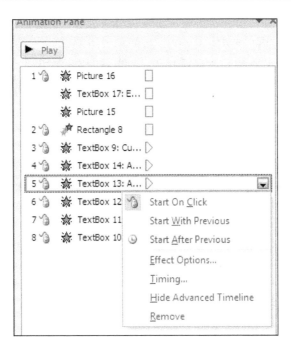

These additional animations are added in the same way that the first animation was added in the main part of this recipe.

Additional animations will show up in the list in the order in which they were added. They will also play in this order.

Checking your animations

To check your animation, you can click on the **Play** button at the top of the **Animation** pane. If you would like to run it as a slide slow, you will need to click on the **Slide Show** icon, which is located in the information bar at the bottom of the PowerPoint window, as shown in the following screenshot:

A word about style

Your viewers are not going to be impressed by presentations filled with too many animations that are all too common. Therefore, it is of utmost importance to use animations with discretion. They are a great way to add additional objects to a slide, if they can do so without being a distraction.

Adding audio narration to your slides

Articulate Presenter allows the use of two different types of audio in your presentation. The first is the audio track, which provides background music for your presentation. The second is narration. This program automatically adjusts the volume of your background music whenever there is narration, avoiding competition between the two.

There are two ways of creating your narration in Articulate Presenter, either by recording the narration right into the presentation, or by having your narration recorded professionally and importing it into your presentation. In this section, we will look at how both of these methods are accomplished.

Getting ready

To record narration directly into your presentation, you will need a microphone connected to your computer. It is worthwhile buying a good quality microphone, especially if you are going to be doing a large number of presentations. The sound quality that you can get off a good quality microphone is better than a cheap one.

You don't want to use the microphone that's in your webcam. Not only is this not a high-quality microphone, but the distance between you and the microphone will make you sound like you're speaking from inside a tunnel. Ideally, a microphone should be between three to six inches from your mouth, pointed directly at your mouth. Avoid moving your head from side to side as you speak, as this will make your volume level go up and down. The following are some of the key points to look at before you add an audio narration to your slide:

▸ A windscreen on your microphone is a good investment as it will help prevent the noise from your breathing on it.

▸ You may also want to consider a desktop mic stand so that you don't have to hold it in your hand.

▸ Before recording your narration, it's a good idea to have it written out. Many people think that they can do it off the cuff, but when they get in front of the mic, they forget everything that they were going to say.

▸ A great place to write out your script is in the notes area at the bottom of the PowerPoint screen.

How to do it...

We are going to record the narration directly into the presentation using Articulate Presenter's built-in recording function. Perform the following steps to do so:

1. Before recording your narration, you need to ensure that your presentation is ready to receive your recording. To do this, open the **Presentation Options** dialog box from the **Articulate** ribbon. On the **Other** tab, make sure that the **Show notes pane on narration window** and **Record narration for one slide at a time** checkboxes under the **Recording** section are both checked, as shown in the following screenshot:

2. Open the recording screen by clicking on the **Record Narration** button in the **Narration** section of the **Articulate** ribbon. If you have not yet saved your presentation, you will be asked to do so before the **Record Narration** screen opens.

Your PowerPoint screen will seem to disappear when you open the recording screen. Don't worry, you haven't lost it; when you finish recording your narration, it will appear again. If you are using multiple monitors for your computer, the **Narration** recording screen will always appear on the far right monitor. So if you have something there that you will need to access, you may want to move it before entering the record mode.

3. To begin recording, click on the **START RECORDING** button on the **Articulate** ribbon.

4. While you are recording, the **START RECORDING** button changes to **STOP RECORDING**. When you have finished recording the narration for the slide, click on the **STOP RECORDING** button.

If you click on the **START RECORDING** button again after you've stopped recording, it will start the recording again, overwriting what you just recorded. As you are recording, the length of the recording you are making will show in the yellow message bar and will be broken down into hours, minutes, seconds, and tenths of a second.

5. You can check your recording using the **Play** and **Stop** buttons to the right-hand side of the **START RECORDING** button. These buttons are identified with the standard graphical symbols for play and record.

6. Now that you have recorded the narration for the first slide, you can move to the next slide using the right and left arrow buttons to the right-hand side of the **Record** and **Play** buttons. You can also select which slide to edit using the drop-down menu located below these buttons.

7. To the right-hand side of the **Play** and **Record** buttons, there is an area for selecting the slide that you want to record the narration for. To verify which slides you have already recorded, click on the small arrow pointing downwards below the slide number in the ribbon. This will open a dropbox with a list of all the slides and thumbnails. All the slides that have a narration recorded will show a small icon of a microphone. Above this, they will tell you the duration of the narration that you have recorded, as shown in the following screenshot:

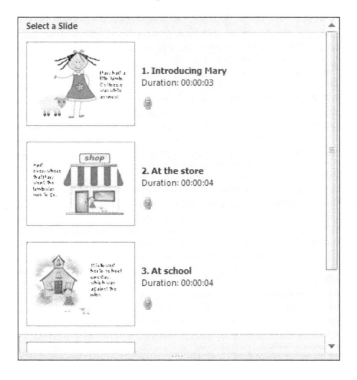

8. To exit the narration recorder and return to PowerPoint, click on the **Save & Close** button on the ribbon.

How it works...

Your narrations will be saved in a new file, which has the same name as you gave your presentation, with the .ppta filename extension. The file will be automatically created at this time, if the program has not already created it. If you have to move your presentation for any reason, be sure to move this file along with the .ppta file, which is the presentation. Otherwise you will lose your narrations.

There's more...

Not only can you record narrations, but you can also import them into the presentation. You may choose to do this using professional "voice" for a specific voice style or for a more professional presentation.

Importing narrations into your presentation

If you decide to use professionally recorded narrations using professional talent, you will probably not be able to record them with Articulate's recorder. This isn't a problem, as you can very easily import those recordings into your presentation.

There are some technical requirements for your recordings. They must be recorded in either the .wav or .mp3 format. Between the two, you are better off using the .wav format files as they are not compressed like the .mp3 files. This means that your finished presentation will be a bigger file, but it will provide a better sound quality for editing. They must be recorded at a sampling rate of 44.1 kHz, 16-bit resolution, and either stereo or mono. Many recording studios and artists prefer to use a resolution of 32 bits, however if you attempt to import 32-bit files into an Articulate presentation, all you will hear is a screech. Perform the following steps for importing narrations:

1. To import these files, click on the **Import Audio** button in the **Narration** section of the **Articulate** ribbon. This will open the **Import Audio** dialog box. This dialog box contains a simple chart showing the slide numbers, the slide names, and the audio track for the narration. If you have recorded a narration for a slide, it will state the existing narration; if you have no narration, this column will be empty.

2. Select the slide that you wish to import an audio file to by clicking on it. Then click on the **Browse...** button at the bottom of the screen. This will open a standard, Windows open file dialog box, where you can search for and select your audio file for that particular narration.

3. You can select multiple narration files to be imported at once. Simply select the first file you need in the Windows open file dialog box, then hold down the *Shift* key and select the last. If the files are not sequentially located in the folder, you can hold down the *Ctrl* key, select each file individually, and then import them all together.

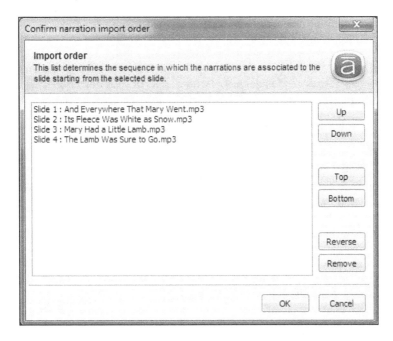

4. When you do this, a new dialog box will open, allowing you to put the audio files in their correct order. The list of files will be shown in the central part of the dialog box. To change the order, select the file you wish to move, and use the **Up**, **Down**, **Top**, **Bottom**, and **Reverse** buttons on the right-hand side of the dialog box to move them as you need to.

If you do not get the order of your narration files correct in the dialog box, you will need to individually change the audio files associated with the slides, as there is no way of moving them around in the **Import Audio** dialog box.

Editing audio

Rarely does it work out that the recording of a narration comes out perfect. While it may be usable, there is always the opportunity for improvement. While you may not think the audio is anywhere near as important as the graphics you use on your slides, poor quality audio can become a distraction, especially if the volume is too low to be clearly audible.

Knowing this, the creators of Articulate have built a simple but very capable audio editor. With it you can easily overcome any deficiencies in the quality of your narration, taking mediocre recordings and turning them into something that sounds as if it came out of a professional recording studio.

Getting ready

To edit the audio, you'll need to have a PowerPoint presentation with some audio. You can use the same presentation where you added the narration, as we saw in the previous recipe. If you did not save that presentation, make a short presentation and record the narration for it so that you'll have something to work with.

I've been using the three-slide presentation of "Mary Had a Little Lamb", which we created for *Chapter 1, Getting Started with Articulate Suite*. I added narration to these slides, reading the text off them. This is the audio that we will be editing.

How to do it...

For editing audio perform the following steps:

1. Quality comes from paying attention to details. That's really what editing is about, taking care of details. We're going to use Articulate Presenter's sound editor to verify and correct the quality of the narration we've recorded. Click on the **Audio Editor** button in the **Narration** section of the **Articulate** ribbon, as shown in the following screenshot:

   The **Audio Editor** window looks quite simple, but has a number of very important functions, which help ensure the quality of your presentation. The main part of the screen is showing the waveform of the sound file that you recorded. These are separated by vertical lines that represent each slide, as follows:

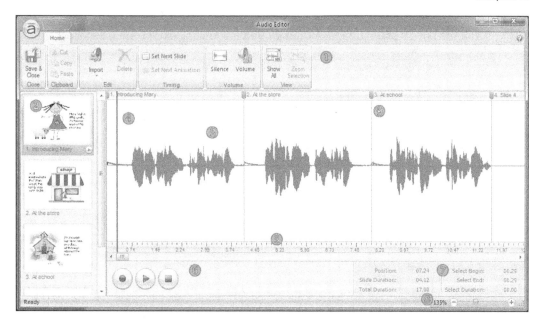

 Volume levels on narrations are very important. If the sound is too low, the listener may not be able to hear it. If it is too high, it will distort. Consistency is also important, as a narration that varies from slide to slide or from one part of your presentation to another is distracting and annoying.

2. The first thing we want to look at is the adjustment of the volume level. Typically, your recorded narration will not be at a high enough volume level. The editor allows you to change this volume level, maximizing it for your audience. Before amplifying the volume, you will need to select the part of the waveform that needs to be amplified or the entire waveform. Select the part of the waveform that you wish to affect by clicking-and-dragging it, clicking at one end and holding the *Shift* key and clicking at the other end, or pressing *Ctrl + A* on the keyboard to select the entire waveform across the entire presentation.

3. Once you have selected the waveform that needs to be amplified, click on the **Volume** button of the ribbon. A **Change Volume** dialog box will open, as follows:

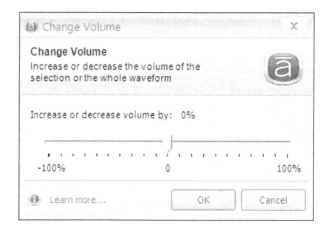

4. Adjust the slider to change the volume level. The same dialog box allows you to both increase and decrease the volume level. Increasing it to **100%** will double the actual volume level of the waveform (3 dB increase). Decreasing it to **-100%** will cut the volume level in half (3 dB reduction). Make a note of the amount of your increase or decrease, in case you need to do it later to another slide.

5. You might need to trim off the excess recording time at the beginning and end of the narration. In this example, we can see that there is about half a second of silence before and after the narration. You can eliminate this excess time by highlighting the area you wish to remove and clicking on the *Delete* key on your keyboard.

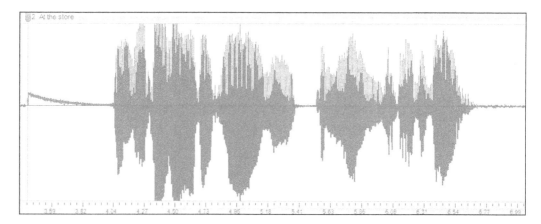

6. In addition to removing unwanted silence, you can use **Audio Editor** in the same way to remove unwanted sounds. Coughs, movement noises, turning pages, and the inadvertent sounds such as "um" and "ah" that we all tend to make sound very unprofessional. To listen to your recording and locate these sounds, use the **Play** and **Stop** buttons below the waveform.

7. Sometimes it can be difficult to isolate these sounds in the waveform. To make it easier to visually separate the good narration from these sounds, magnify the time line using the slider in the lower-right corner of the dialog box.

8. To delete these sounds once you have located them, highlight them in the same manner that you highlighted the silence in step 5. Then eliminate them by clicking on **Delete** in the ribbon.

9. In the case where there may not be enough time for the viewer to read and absorb the material on the slide, you can add silence. In the preceding waveform, there is a short pause between two separate sentences. We can extend that pause by adding silence, as shown in the following screenshot:

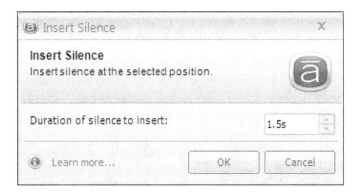

10. To add a time of silence to your narration waveform, select the point where you want the silence to go. The red cursor line should go to that point, indicating that you are at the point where you want to be. Click on the **Silence** button on the ribbon, and the **Insert Silence** dialog box will appear, allowing you to add the amount of silence in seconds, which you want to add to your narration. Simply type the number in and click on the **OK** button.

How it works...

Ideally you want the waveform to fill as much of the vertical space as possible, without hitting the top and bottom edges of the waveform area. When the waveform is too small, you probably won't have enough volume even if you boost the volume as much as possible on your computer or video projector. However, if you make the volume so high that it hits the top and bottom edges of the window, the audio will start "clipping", a type of distortion, which will make the narration harder to understand, as shown in the following screenshot:

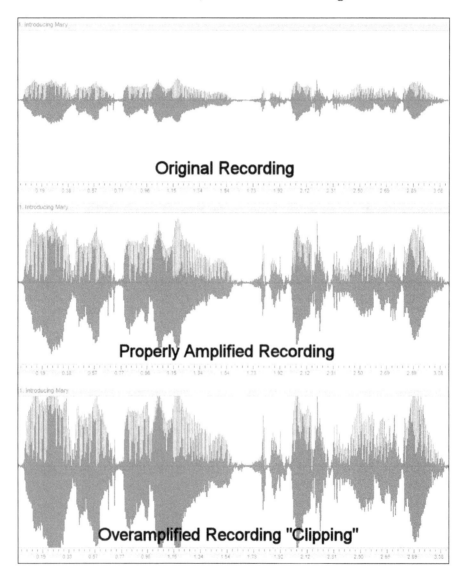

As long as you can still see a little bit of whitespace above and below the peaks of the waveform, you haven't overamplified it. However, you only want to see a little bit of it. It may be necessary to amplify your narration in stages, in order to get it to the proper volume level. In this example, we have amplified the original recording with the maximum possible value, that is twice, to reach the proper volume level.

If you overamplify and find yourself in a position where the waveform is clipping, you are better off undoing your amplification and trying again with a lower setting, instead of reducing the overamplified waveform. Even though you reduce it again, you will not undo the clipping by reducing the volume; you will just lower the volume of the clipping.

As a digital waveform, the narration will not get distorted by amplifying it unless you get to the point of clipping. However, you must keep in mind that everything will amplify, such as your voice, the sound of a fan running in your office, the dog barking outside, and your noisy watch. Anything that is included in the waveform will be amplified by the same percentage that you are amplifying your narration with.

For this reason, it is very important to do your recording in an extremely quiet atmosphere. Many people think it's quiet just because nobody is talking, but this isn't true. People walking, opening file cabinet drawers, and air conditioning systems can all create noise that is unacceptable in your recording.

There's more...

Audio Editor in Articulate Presenter is a fairly powerful tool, which provides a number of different options so that you can provide the best possible narration for your presentation.

Adjusting the view of the waveform

If it is necessary to adjust the size of your narration waveform in order to be able to see all of it or part of it, there are three ways in which you can do this:

- Use the **Show All** and **Zoom Selection** buttons in the **View** section of the ribbon. These allow you to either condense the waveform to the width of the window in the **Audio Editor** window or zoom out to a selection that you have chosen.
- Use the view magnification slider at the bottom of the **Audio Editor** window.
- Use the scroll wheel on your mouse.

Changing the magnification of the view does not in any way change the waveform, just how it is presented to you. It doesn't change your view of the amplitude either (the volume level shown in the vertical direction), but only changes the time line scale, allowing you to see more or less of the waveform.

Typically, it is necessary to increase the magnification when working on particular parts of the waveform. When done, you might want to zoom back to a full view in order to see everything and make sure that you didn't forget to make some changes.

Recording narration

Although it is actually easier to record your narration on the **Record Narration** screen, you might find times when you want to record here in **Audio Editor**, especially if you need to modify a narration. Let's say that you have left out a sentence in your narration and notice that while reviewing it, or you notice a door closing in the background. Instead of re-recording the entire narration, you could correct it here by performing the following steps:

1. To record an addition to your narration or to re-record a section, start by placing the cursor where you want to insert the new recording.

2. Prepare your microphone and mentally rehearse what you are going to say.

3. Use the red record button on the bottom of the **Audio Editor** to start and stop your recording. The **Audio Editor** will insert this new recording into your waveform, moving everything after that point over, to allow it to fit in.

4. If this recording is to replace some part of your existing narration, you will need to highlight and delete the old section of the waveform. To best ensure that your new recording matches the existing narration, there are some things you need to do, as follows:

   - Record the new narration at the same time of day as your old narration. Voices change throughout the day both in volume levels and in tone. If you recorded in the morning and re-recorded in the evening, your voice will not match.

   - Record with the same microphone and audio settings. Different microphones record differently. Using a different microphone may not make you sound like a different person, but the difference will be noticeable.

   - Ensure that you have eliminated the background noises.

Importing narration

You can also import audio files if you have had your narration recorded in an actual sound studio with professional talent.

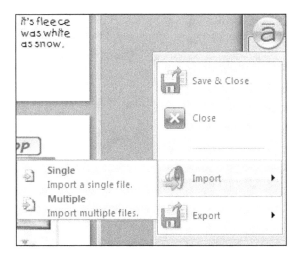

To import your narration perform the following steps:

1. Open the **Audio Editor** window, click on the **Articulate** button at the upper-left corner, then click on **Import**, and then choose **Single** or **Multiple** files. When you select **Import** from the menu, a fly-out menu will appear asking if you want to import a single or multiple audio files.

   Remember that you can only import .wav and .mp3 audio files into Articulate.

2. If you select **Single**, a dialog box opens asking where you would like to import the audio file. Select the appropriate location and click on the **OK** button, which will cause **Audio Editor** to complete the import:

3. If you select **Multiple**, a different dialog box opens, allowing you to select the slides you want to import the multiple files to. In there you will see thumbnails of the various slides in your presentation, along with a notation for those that already have an existing narration.

4. Select the slide that you want the narration to be imported to, and then click on the **Browse...** button. This opens a standard, Windows open file dialog box where you can select the file for that slide. Once all the audio files are selected, click on the **OK** button to import them.

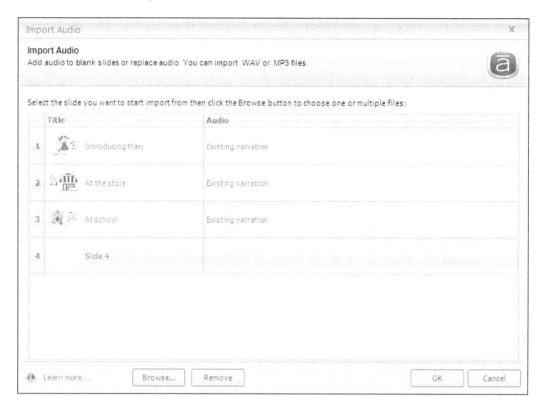

You need to use some caution here. If you accidentally select a slide where you already have a narration, it will replace that narration with the new file. This action is not reversible.

Exporting narration

Should you need to use the narration you have recorded for your Articulate presentation apart from the presentation, you can also export it using the **Articulate** button. Articulate will automatically save the audio file with the slide's name, making it easy to identify.

Exporting could be useful to you if you need to use the same narration in multiple presentations. Let's say that you are doing several versions of an educational presentation about a particular product, one for technical people, another for management, and another for sales in general. Some of the slides will overlap along with their narrations. By exporting the narrations from the first presentation, you can easily import them into the others, saving yourself time and hassle. To export the narration perform the following steps:

1. Click on the **Articulate** button in the upper-left corner of the **Audio Editor** window.

2. In the menu select **Export**. This will open a fly-out menu, where you can select the format that you want the file to be saved in.

3. Once you have selected the format, a standard, Windows browse dialog box will appear, allowing you to select the location.

Adding background music to your presentation

When you watch a movie, do you notice the background music? If you're like most of us, you probably don't unless there's some really dramatic music at one point or another. We might notice the introductory theme music, but after that most of us don't pay much attention to the music, although it is an important part of any movie scene. It is the music more than anything, which sets the scene, telling us if it's going to be suspenseful, romantic, humorous, or sad.

Adding background music to your presentation has the same affect. The right music can have a lot to do with how the viewer receives the message you are presenting, whether for a corporate proposal or for the training session of a sales message. Selecting and adding your music is an important part of creating the total effect of your presentation.

This is one of the places where we want to do the work from Articulate instead of PowerPoint, even though PowerPoint has the capacity to add music. However, if you add it through PowerPoint, it will not get into your Flash video presentation.

Getting ready

You will need a presentation that you can work with. It doesn't matter if you work with an existing presentation or create a couple of slides just for using them in this recipe.

How to do it...

Background music isn't something that is created or recorded in Articulate Presenter, but rather prerecorded music that is imported into the presentation. It must be imported into a playlist so that Articulate can use it. Perform the following steps to do so:

1. The playlist library is created in the **Presentation Options** section, which can be found on the **Articulate** ribbon, as shown in the following screenshot:

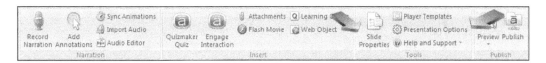

2. Click on the **Playlists** tab in the **Presentation Options** dialog box to access the playlists.

3. At the top of the dialog box, there is a drop-down menu where you can select a playlist from your existing playlists. Click on the button below this box, which says **New...**.

4. Another dialog box will open, where you can type in the name of your playlist. Once you find it, click on the **OK** button.

5. Verify that the new playlist name that you created is showing in the **Playlist** drop-down list. If not, open the list and select it.

6. The middle part of the dialog box is where you add music to the playlist. Clicking on the **Add...** button opens a standard, Windows open file dialog box, where you can select the music that you want to add to the playlist. Click on the file and then click the **Open** button.

7. Music files will play in the order in which they are listed in the playlist. There are buttons to the right of the list, which can be used for adjusting the order.

   Don't forget that the only two types of audio files that Articulate accepts are `.wav` and `mp3`. If your music tracks are not already in one of these formats, you will need to convert them before attempting to import them into your playlist. There are a number of freeware and open source, audio file converters available on the Internet. One that works extremely well is Audacity, which is available for free at `www.audacity.sourceforge.net`.

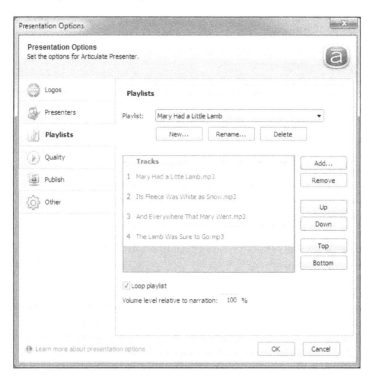

8. Below the list of music that is in your playlist is a checkbox for **Loop playlist**. Checking this causes the playlist to be repeated over and over, as long as it is selected for one or all slides. This will continue until the **Loop playlist** checkbox is deselected or the playlist is replaced by another playlist.

9. The final setting is **Volume level relative to narration**. You set this by typing in the textbox. For best results it should be 25 to 30.

10. Click on the **OK** button to close the dialog box. Your playlist will be saved automatically.

11. Once your playlists are created, they need to be added to the slides in your presentation. To do so click on the **Slide Properties** button, which can be found on the **Articulate** ribbon:

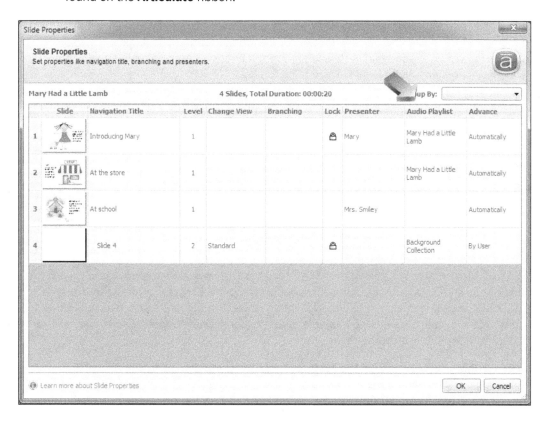

12. The **Slide Properties** dialog box consists of a chart for selecting a number of attributes for each individual slide. Thumbnails of the slides appear along the left-hand side of the table, allowing you to quickly and easily identify which slides you are working on. Almost all the way to the right-hand side in this dialog box is a column titled **Audio Playlist**. Clicking on one of the cells in this column opens a drop-down list of the available playlists.

How it works...

This is a library, so it is not specific to any one presentation. You can have an unlimited number of playlists in your library. If you are creating a series of training courses that go together, you may want to use the same playlists throughout the series to create continuity and "branding".

Multiple playlists can be used in one presentation, so there is no need to try and create a playlist that exactly matches your presentation, with the types of music exactly matching the mood you want to create for each slide. Instead, you can create several different playlists, each of which matches a certain "mood".

When selecting music for your playlists, keep in mind both the mood you want to create and the length of the piece of music. While there is no problem with looping, having the same piece loop over and over again can become boring. On the other hand, using music that is too long can cause the overall file size to be too big.

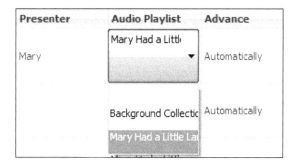

As you can see from the screenshot of the dialog box, we have selected the same playlist for the first two slides, skipped the third slide, and used a different playlist for the fourth slide. This will cause the first playlist to continue being played through the first two slides, without interruption. If you have selected **Loop playlist**, the looping will happen at whatever moment is necessary, ignoring whichever slide it is in.

Once the third slide is reached, the **Mary Had a Little Lamb** playlist would stop and there would not be any background music for this slide. On the fourth slide, a new playlist would start.

There's more...

The **Volume level relative to narration** option establishes what volume level you want Articulate to drop your background music to, when narration begins. The program will fade the volume level down to that level for the duration of the narration and then fade it back up again to full volume, as follows:

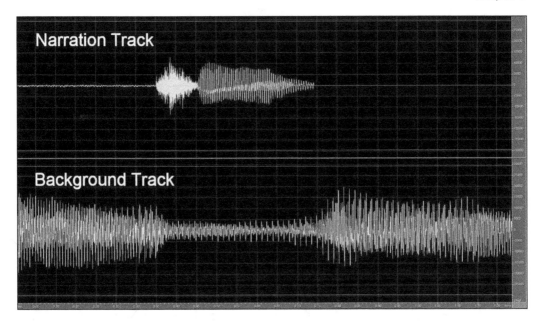

Narration Track

Background Track

While you can set this level to whatever value you want, you will want to be sure that the narration can be clearly heard over the background music. To do this, a level of 25 to 30 percent works well. Anything softer makes the music seem to disappear, while anything louder can make it hard to understand the words that are being spoken.

This volume level needs to be individually set for each playlist. Setting it for one does not automatically set it for all. When you are done, click on the **OK** button and your settings will be saved.

Keep in mind that other than the adjustment of volume for narration, which we've already mentioned, Articulate doesn't have any capability of editing your background music tracks. If you need to adjust the dynamics, add effects, or even add sound effects, you will need to do that in another program before importing the songs into your playlist.

Syncing the animations with narrations

Although we set up the animations in PowerPoint, we've got to sync them to the narration in Articulate. Remember that we're creating a Flash video presentation, so we really can't make it in a way that the viewer clicks on the mouse button to start the animation sequence, even though we told PowerPoint that we wanted the animations to start on a mouse click.

In most presentations, the animations need to run at a particular point in time to match the narration. So what we are going to do is sync them with the narration. In the Flash video presentation, the animations will run automatically as part of the presentation. What we're going to do at this point is tell them when to run.

Getting ready

Obviously, we have to have the animations set up themselves, before we can accomplish this stage. We discussed that earlier in this chapter, so we're not going to repeat it now. If you are not sure how to set up your animations, please go back and review the *Animating images and objects* recipe in this chapter.

How to do it...

Syncing the animations with narrations is one of those details that makes the difference between an average presentation and one that truly looks professional. It is worth taking the time to get the syncing of the animations perfect, so that the viewer will not be distracted by differences in timing between the animation and the narration. Perform the following steps to do so:

1. The button for syncing the animations is found in the **Narration** section of the **Articulate** ribbon. Clicking on it will open the same screen that was used for recording your narrations. The one thing that will look different is that the drop-down menu all the way on the left-hand side will show **Sync Animations** instead of **Record Narration**, as shown in the following screenshot:

   Don't worry if your slide appears blank. Remember that you're working on syncing your animations. If everything on the slide is supposed to come in via an animation, you will start out with a blank slide.

2. Check to see that the button in the ribbon that had previously said **START RECORDING** now says **START SYNC** and the yellow message bar says **Press 'Start Sync' to sync animations**. If you don't have any animations for that slide, the message will be **No animations for this slide**:

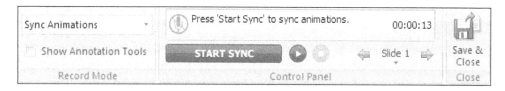

   It is important to pay attention to this message. If you try and sync your animations without having any animations selected for the slide, Articulate will automatically switch over to the record animation mode. You will end up recording over your previous animation. There is no undo for this action.

3. Articulate has you sync the animation one slide at a time. To select the slide, use the arrows to the right-hand side of the **START SYNC** button.

4. To sync the animation for a slide, click on the **START SYNC** button. The slide narration will start playing immediately and the **START SYNC** button will change to **Next Animation**. The yellow information bar will tell you how many animations you have left for that slide.

5. As the narration plays, click on the mouse button at the point where you want each animation to occur. When you are done, click on the mouse button once more to end the animation sequence.

6. Check your animation by using the graphic **Play** and **Stop** buttons to the right-hand side of the **START SYNC** button.

7. Once you are satisfied with the animations for all your slides, you can click on the **Save & Close** button to exit the **Sync Animation** screen and return to viewing your presentation in PowerPoint.

8. The fine-tuning of your animation sync is done in the **Audio Editor** window of Articulate. You will find the button to open the **Audio Editor** window in the **Narration** section of the **Articulate** ribbon:

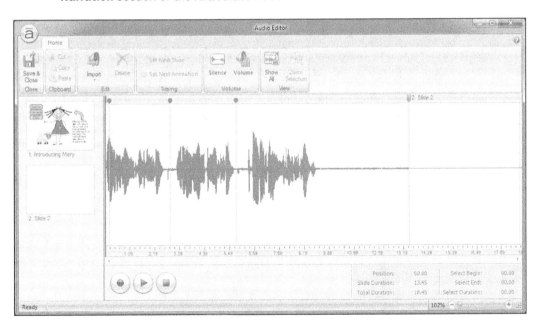

9. Locate the three, dotted, vertical lines in the middle of the central pane of the editor, all of which have a round blue handle at the top. These are the points that you set the animations to, to start in the **Sync Animations** screen.

10. Hover your mouse cursor over one of these handles. The cursor will change from a single arrow to a double-headed arrow. Click on the mouse and drag to move the animation's position along the waveform.

How it works...

In the **Audio Editor** window, you will see a waveform of the slide you are working on. Along the left-hand side is a series of thumbnails, which allows you to select the slide that you want to work on. They are the **Record**, **Play**, and **Stop** buttons at the bottom of the window, allowing you to record directly into the editor and play back your narration to hear it.

If you look at the waveform, you will see that it gets very active and then stops, and then gets very active and then stops again. Each area of activity represents some place where the narrator is talking. Each flat line in the waveform represents the silence of the narrator. There are also five vertical lines running through the waveform.

The red line is the cursor. If you play the audio narration, it will move along the waveform, letting you know exactly where you are at any point in time. The line all the way to the right-hand side of the waveform is the stop line. That tells the program when the narration stops. As you can see in the screenshot, there are a few seconds of silence in this waveform before the sound stops. That can be eliminated by just moving the end line over.

The three lines in the middle are the points of the animation, which we've already discussed. They can be moved by grabbing the handle at the top with your mouse cursor and dragging it.

If you notice in the screenshot, the first animation is starting just after the audio waveform starts, the second one is right in the center of the silence, and the third is a little before the center of the silence. My intent was to have the first animation start right at the beginning of the narration, but I couldn't click that fast. So I'll move the line over, adjusting its timing:

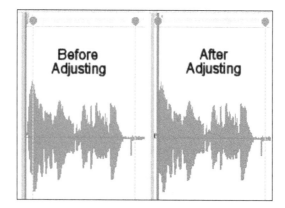

While the difference isn't all that big, it can be an important one, especially when you have several transitions and you're trying to make them line up with certain text in your narration. We normally find ourselves fine-tuning the sync of our animations even if it's only to adjust the start time of the first animation, to be as close to the beginning of the narration as we can be.

You can still perform this fine-tuning even if you don't have any narration for the slide. Just remember that the length of time, which you will have, will be as whatever you set the default slide time to in the **Publish** tab of the **Presentation Options** dialog box. If you did not change this, the program default for the amount of time that a file is shown for is five seconds.

There's more...

The way that we just synced our animations is the common way of doing so in Articulate Presenter. However, there are some other options for adjusting the animation timing.

Adding animation timings in the Audio Editor

In addition to moving the timing of the animations, the ribbon has two buttons in the **Timing** section that are **Set Next Slide** or **Set Next Animation**.

These two buttons will be grayed out when they can't be used. That would be because of not having another animation for that slide or not having another slide in the presentation. Perform the following steps:

1. To add another animation on a slide, click on the waveform at the point where you would like to add the animation. The red cursor should move to that point.

2. Click on the **Set Next Animation** button in the **Timing** section of the ribbon. This will create a new animation timing mark.

3. You can adjust the position of these animations and slide transitions, just as you could with the animations you put in through the **Animation Sync** screen.

4. To add a slide transition point, click on the waveform where you want the transition to happen. The red cursor line should move to that point.

5. Click on the **Set Next Slide** button in the **Timing** section of the ribbon. A slide transition mark should appear on the time line.

See also

▸ The *Animating images and objects* recipe

Adding video to your course

There may be times when you want to add video to your training course or presentation. Video is a great way of presenting a lot of information quickly, which can save you a number of slides in your presentation. At the same time, you need to realize that adding video to your presentation will make the file size considerably larger. This may cause bandwidth problems, especially for people who have dial-up connections.

As a software package creating Flash video, Articulate can only work with Flash videos created in the `.flv`, `.mp4`, or `.swf` formats. If your videos are in any other format, you will need to convert them.

Getting ready

Since we are adding video, we'll need a course to add them to. Open a presentation that you can work with or create a short one by adding some text and images to at least one slide. You can either leave room on that slide for the video or add the video to another slide.

How to do it...

To add video to your course perform the following steps:

1. Video, like all forms of media used with Articulate, needs to be added from the **Articulate** ribbon and not in the normal way that it is done in PowerPoint. To import videos, click on the **Flash Movie** icon in the **Insert** section of the **Articulate** ribbon. This will open a standard, Windows open file dialog box, where you can select the video that you want to insert into your presentation.

2. Once you select the video and click on **OK**, the **Insert Flash Movie** dialog box will open, showing a thumbnail of the video you have selected.

3. To make sure that you have selected the correct video, you can preview it right from the dialog buttons by using the **Play** and **Stop** buttons, which are located below the thumbnail. On the left-hand side below the thumbnail, it shows the length of the video in minutes and seconds along with a counter that shows where in the play sequence the video is while it is running:

4. Articulate doesn't actually insert the video at this point in time, but rather waits until you are publishing the presentation. A place marker will be used to indicate the location of the video.

5. Select when the presentation will advance to the next slide, by selecting **Automatically when the movie finishes** for the **Advance to the next slide** drop-down menu.

6. In the drop-down list for **Synchronization**, select **Synchronize slide and movie**.

7. Once your video selection is complete and your settings have been made, click on the **OK** button to place the video placeholder on your slide.

How it works...

Remember that changing the size of your video can change its clarity. If your video is smaller than the size that you wish to present it with, it will affect the image quality, showing the video to be pixelated.

If you select to place your video in the presenter panel, the placeholder will only be an icon in the upper-left corner of the slide. If you choose to have your video displayed in a new browser window, the placeholder will also be an icon, but this time it will be located in the lower-right corner of the slide.

The lower controls in the dialog box will change depending upon which selection you make for the display location. **Display in presenter panel** will eliminate the option for synchronization while **Display in new browser window** will eliminate both, instead of asking which browser controls you want to allow.

There is one important detail you need to realize about videos in Articulate Presenter. As the presentation is running, Articulate is loading the presentation into its memory two slides ahead of the slide that the viewer is watching. So if lengthy videos are placed in the first two slides, they may not load well and may take a pause during their presentation. This problem can be easily rectified by having at least two introductory slides before any video, as follows:

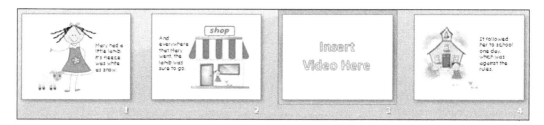

If you are inserting the video in the slide, this place marker will be the size of the recorded video. You can place, move, and stretch the size of the placeholder box, which will affect the size of your video. Although it is possible to change the size of your video, it is not recommended as it can cause distortion of the video.

You can select for the slide to advance after the video ends or upon mouse click. If you select it to advance automatically, then the slide will not change until the video ends, regardless of whether the narration is completed or not. Regardless of which one you choose, the viewer always has the option of changing the slide even in the midst of the video.

There's more...

There are three play options for videos to choose from. You have three choices shown by the three radio buttons in the middle of the **Insert Flash Movie** dialog box. These choices are as follows:

- **Display in slide**: This allows you to present the video as part of the presentation, in the main part of the slide.

- **Display in presenter panel**: This is the panel in the skin that shows who is presenting the training. This allows you to use a video in place of a photograph for the presenter. This video will be displayed at 244 pixels in width. Please note that this is not part of the presentation itself, but the presenter skin sidebar (see the following screenshot).

- **Display in new browser window**: This will cause a new browser window to open, where the video will play automatically so that your viewer can see it. While this does allow for larger video sizes, it means that the viewer will have to navigate back to your presentation once the video is completed.

Video Playback Settings

1. The last setting in the **Insert Flash Video** dialog box is for synchronization. This determines whether the movie is considered a part of the slide's timeline or not. By selecting **Synchronize slide and movie**, the slide's runtime will be added to the seek bar in the control bar section of the presentation. This allows the viewer to repeat sections of the video, if they so desire, by selecting a point on the seek bar.

2. If you choose to have the movie playing independently from the slide, it loses control of the ability to repeat sections of the video. However, you then have the option of delaying the start of the movie.

3. To tell Articulate to delay the beginning of the video, select **Movie Plays Independently of Slide** from the **Synchronization** drop-down menu.

4. Once you select that, the line at the bottom of the dialog box that says **Start Flash movie...** turns from gray to black. Insert the number of seconds you want the video delayed by in the textbox.

Video formatting

Articulate Office '09 comes with a Video Encoder program that can change your videos from other formats to the .flv format. We will discuss how to do this in *Chapter 5, Taking Your Quiz to the Next Level* of this book.

It is important to remember that Articulate Presenter '09 needs Flash videos to be in version 3.0.79 or above. If you are using the .swf files, they need to be created with **ActionScript 2.0 (AC2)**. For .mp4 videos, they need to be encoded with the H.264 codec.

Regardless of what else you place on the slide, the video will always be layered on top of any other items. You cannot move it towards the back or place objects over it. This means that you cannot use any sort of video overlays, frames, or annotations on top of your video.

Multiple videos

It is possible to insert up to three Flash movies into an Articulate slide. Even so, this is not normally recommended as it can slow the presentation down depending on the computer that the presentation is being run on and the Internet connection (when being downloaded from the Internet).

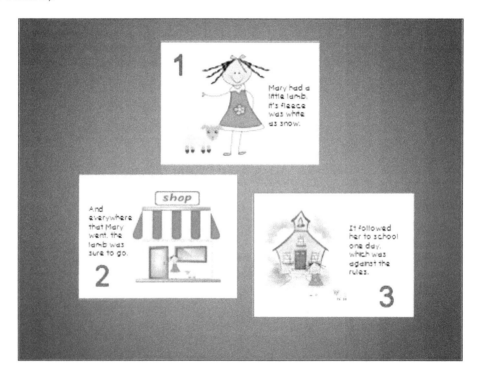

Additional videos are added in exactly the same way that the first video was added.

▸   *Chapter 5, Taking Your Quiz to the Next Level*

Adding video from the Web

There may be times when you want to add a video from the Web to your presentation, rather than something that is available locally. There is a lot of good video content on websites such as YouTube and Vimeo, many of which are useful for training and other purposes.

Getting ready

You'll need a presentation that you can add a video into. If you still have the presentation that you used in the last recipe, you can continue working with it.

How to do it...

Any video that can be accessed online can be added to your Articulate presentation, and not just those that are available on YouTube and Vimeo. To add a video from the Web, perform the following steps:

1. You will find the **Web Object** button in the **Insert** section of the **Articulate** ribbon. Clicking on this button opens the **Insert Web Object** dialog box:

2. This is a fairly straightforward dialog box that allows you to create a hyperlink to the web object and make the necessary settings to have it functioning in your Articulate Flash video:

3. The first thing you see is a place to insert the URL of the video that you wish to insert into your presentation. The easiest way to fill this in is to find the website with the video, copy the URL directly off your browser, and paste it here.

4. Always use the **Test Link** button to verify that you have copied the address of the video correctly. Taking a moment to do this can prevent you from having to redo the task later.

5. We have the option of having a web-based video show in the slide or opening it in a new browser window. Select the radio button next to **Display in slide** to make the video display in the presentation slide rather than displaying it in a new browser window.

6. To determine when the presenter advances to the next slide, select **When user clicks next** from the **Advance to the next slide** drop-down list.

7. We want to delay the starting of the video by five seconds after the slide begins, in order to accommodate some narration. To do so, type the number 5 in the **Show after** textbox, as shown in the following screenshot:

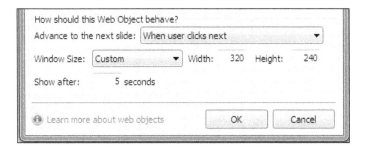

8. As we want to change the size of the video, select **Custom** from the drop-down list next to **Window Size**. This will open additional textboxes in the same dialog box, where you need to type in the size in pixels. Let's set **Width** to 320 pixels and **Height** to 240 pixels.

How it works...

Just as with adding videos, you must add web-based videos to your presentation through Articulate and not through PowerPoint. Videos added through PowerPoint will not be displayed as part of your Flash presentation.

Articulate Presenter treats these videos as web objects. While they are not actually imported into your presentation, they are accessed directly from your presentation. This means that you need to have an Internet connection when you use any presentation that contains these videos.

The default size for videos is 320 x 240 pixels, which is the old standard for web-based video. It has a 4:3 aspect ratio. However, many recent videos are created in HD at a 17:9 aspect ratio. You must be sure that the dimensions you set for the custom size video are compatible with the video format you are using. This includes both the aspect ratio and overall size.

There's more...

What we did in this recipe puts the URL of the web page into the presentation. To make sure that you get just the video and not the web page, you will need to find the URL that is specific to the video rather than the web page. This process is slightly different for each website that you can get the video off.

Videos from YouTube

YouTube makes adding the videos easy, with a built-in function that is accessible from their context-sensitive menu. Perform the following steps:

1. For YouTube, find the video you want to use and right-click on it. A context-sensitive menu will appear where you can select **Copy video URL**. By inserting this as the address on the **Insert Web Object** dialog box, you can have just the video appear in your presentation.

```
Copy video URL
Copy video URL at current time
Pop out
Copy embed html
Report playback issue
Take speed test
Stop download
Show video info
Copy debug info

Settings...
Global Settings...
About Adobe Flash Player 11.2.202.228...
```

2. To paste the URL, right-click on the **Address** textbox in the dialog box and select **Paste**. To access the context-sensitive menu, right-click on the **Address** textbox in the dialog box and select **Paste**.

3. An alternate means of pasting is to use the keyboard shortcut, which consists of holding down the *Ctrl* key and typing *V*.

Videos from Vimeo

Like YouTube, Vimeo also makes it easy to use their videos in a wide variety of places, including your Articulate Presentation. Perform the following steps:

1. For Vimeo, the process is almost the same. When you right-click on the video, a context-sensitive menu will appear where you can select **Copy video URL**. The URL for the video in Vimeo will always appear as `http://vimeo.com/` followed by an eight digit number, which identifies the particular video.

2. This URL can be pasted into the **Address** textbox in the **Insert Web Object** dialog box.

```
Watch in Couch Mode on Vimeo

Enter Full Screen
Turn Scaling OFF
Turn Loop ON

Like video
Add to Watch Later

Copy embed code
Copy video URL

Report Slow Loading

Moogaloop Player v5.2.22

Settings...
Global Settings...
About Adobe Flash Player 11.2.202.228...
```

We are not going to provide you with specific instructions for using video from every source on the Internet. However, most of them operate in a similar manner. Always be sure to capture the URL of just the video instead of the page that contains the video. You do not want to use the **Copy embed code** option for this.

Videos from your computer

Although this dialog box deals with inserting web objects, you can actually use other videos that are on your local computer or your local network. The folder icon to the right of the **Address** textbox opens a Windows browse dialog box (slightly different from an open file dialog box) for you to find the local video, whether on your computer or on your network. It can then be selected, putting it in the **Address** textbox.

One of the occasions when you may want to use this is if you have a video that for some reason you don't want to convert to a .flv format. You can put the video into an HTML document on your computer and link to it through this dialog box. Please note that you may have to copy the HTML code and video file into the output folder of the published presentation.

Highlighting specific slide information

There may be times when you wish to highlight certain information on a slide in your presentation. This would usually be due to a need to attract the viewer's eye to specific data or information that you are presenting on the slide. While you can use animations to do this, specifically an Emphasis animation, Articulate Presenter comes with a series of annotation tools to assist you in adding graphic emphasis to your presentation.

These annotation tools are a series of small Flash animations, which can be placed anywhere on your slides. They are somewhat customizable both in their appearance and in the timing of their appearance. This allows you to synchronize the appearance of your annotation to go along with the narration of your slides.

Getting ready

You'll need at least one slide that you can work on for this recipe. Before doing the annotations, it is important to complete your narration and animations. In this way, you can get the maximum impact out of the annotations, timing them to match your narration and having them accentuate your animations. This will help to increase the impact of your overall presentation.

How to do it...

Highlighting is done in the same screen that is used for narrating and syncing your animations. Perform the following steps to highlight specific slide information:

1. You can access the annotation tools by clicking on the **Add Annotations** button in the **Narration** section of the **Articulate** ribbon, as shown in the following screenshot:

2. You will notice three new sections in the ribbon that did not appear when you were recording your narration and setting the timing for your animations. These are the **Annotation**, **Shapes**, and **Style** sections. These sections provide you with the flexibility to create and customize your annotation to meet your presentation's needs.

    You can also access annotations by using the **Add Annotations** drop-down menu on the left-hand side of the ribbon, or by clicking on the checkbox below the drop-down menu that says **Show Annotation Tools**, as shown in the following screenshot:

3. Before beginning to add annotations to your slide, you must determine whether you are going to insert one annotation or multiple annotations. In the part of the ribbon that is in the middle, you will find the **Annotation** section. There are two buttons, one with an arrow on it and the other with three arrows on it (highlighted in the preceding screenshot). Selecting the single arrow button allows only one annotation per slide. Selecting the button with multiple arrows allows you to put multiple annotations into the slide.

 Please note that there is an exception to this, with the **Spotlight** annotation. While you can use the spotlight along with other types of annotations, you can only use one spotlight per slide.

4. Add an arrow annotation to the slide first. Click on the small triangle below the **Arrow** annotation button to open a dropbox where you can make a selection from four different arrow styles, each of which is available, pointing in eight different directions, as shown in the following screenshot:

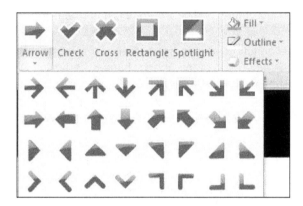

5. Before placing the arrow, change its size by clicking on **Effects** in the **Style** section of the ribbon. In the drop-down menu click on **Size**. Then in the fly-out menu click on **150%**.

6. Animate the annotation by clicking on the **Effects** button in the **Style** section of the ribbon. This time select **Animation** in the menu. Then in the fly-out menu click on **Loop Bounce**.

7. Place the arrow on the slide by clicking where you want it to appear. The placement of the arrow annotation is determined by the point of the arrow; the point will be located where you have clicked.

8. Add a check annotation on the slide by clicking on **Check** in the **Shapes** section of the ribbon.

9. Now click on the **Outlines** section of the ribbon. This opens a dropbox where you can select the outline color for your check annotation.

 All the changes to the basic annotation must be made before placing it. Once it is placed, it cannot be changed. The only change that can be made is to clear all the annotations.

10. The placement of the check annotation is at the inner point of the angle; click on your mouse button with your cursor positioned where you want this angle to be.

11. Add a cross annotation on the slide by clicking on the **Cross** button in the **Shapes** portion of the ribbon. This places an "X" icon on the slide, which can be used to draw attention to something or to show the user if something needs to be crossed out.

12. Click on **Fill** in the **Style** section of the ribbon. This opens a dropbox where you can select the fill color for your check annotation. By clicking on **Semitransparent Fill**, you can place your annotation but still allow the viewer to see what is behind it.

13. Place the cross annotation on the slide by clicking where you want the two lines to cross.

14. Add a rectangle annotation around something on the slide. When you select the rectangle, the **Style** section of the ribbon changes, removing **Fill** and **Effect** while adding **Animation** and **Corners**.

15. Click on the **Corners** button in the **Style** section of the ribbon. The drop-down menu that appears allows you to select straight or rounded corners.

16. To place the rectangle, select one corner of the area with your mouse cursor. Click-and-hold the mouse button and drag to the opposite corner, releasing the button.

17. Add a spotlight annotation to your slide by clicking on the **Spotlight** annotation button in the **Shapes** section of the ribbon.

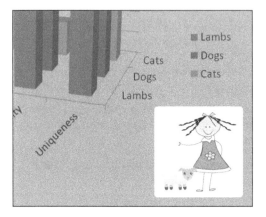

18. To place your spotlight, select one corner of the area that you want spotlighted, outside of the object that you are trying to draw attention to. Click-and-hold your mouse button there. Drag to the opposite corner and release your mouse button. Everything around this rectangle will be grayed out, highlighting whatever is within the rectangle, as shown in the preceding screenshot.

How it works...

All of these annotations can be customized to some extent. The **Style** section allows the changing of fill colors, outline colors, selection of the animation by which the annotation will be drawn into your slide, and the size of the annotation.

It is theoretically possible to insert your annotations at the same time that you are recording your narration. By selecting the checkbox on the **Record Mode** part of the ribbon, you make the **Annotation** section of the ribbon appear during either the **Record Narration** or **Sync Animation** option for this screen. However, it requires incredible agility to be able to juggle both the narration and the annotations. For this reason, it is not recommended.

There's more...

Annotations can be placed either at the beginning of the slide or during the run of the narration. Timing is extremely important when inserting your annotations. Although there is no timeline shown for the running of the slide, annotations are entered into the slide along the timeline of your narration. The **START RECORDING** button, which you used earlier when recording your narration, now says **START ANNOTATION**. Clicking on it would place the selected annotation flash at the point in the narration where you have clicked it.

Timing annotations

To place your annotations at a particular point of time in the narration, you will need to run the narration, placing the annotations as it runs. Getting your timing right for this can be a bit tricky, and unfortunately, you don't get to adjust it afterwards. So it's best to have everything planned out and ready before starting to add your annotations. Perform the following steps to do so:

1. Before starting to add the annotations, mark the locations of the animations in the **Slide Notes** section, marking the words where these annotations will be introduced in bold and noting the annotation itself in parentheses.

2. Click on the **START ANNOTATION** button on the ribbon, which will start playing the narration.

3. When you get to the point in the narration where you want to insert the annotation, stop the narration using the **Pause** button, which is located in the **Control Panel** section of the ribbon. Once you do this, the **START ANNOTATION** button changes to **Resume**.

4. Select the annotation you want and set its color and animation.

5. Place the annotation on the slide at the point where you want it to appear.

6. When you are sure that you have everything ready, click on the **Resume** button, moving on to the next place in the narration where you want to place an annotation on your slide.

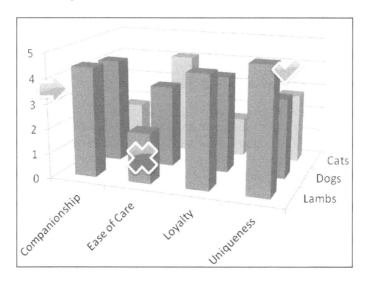

Clearing annotations

In some cases you may want to clear the annotation, especially on longer slides where you might have several annotations. This can be done by clicking on the **Clear All** button in the **Annotation** section of the ribbon. As stated, this will clear all the annotations off your slide:

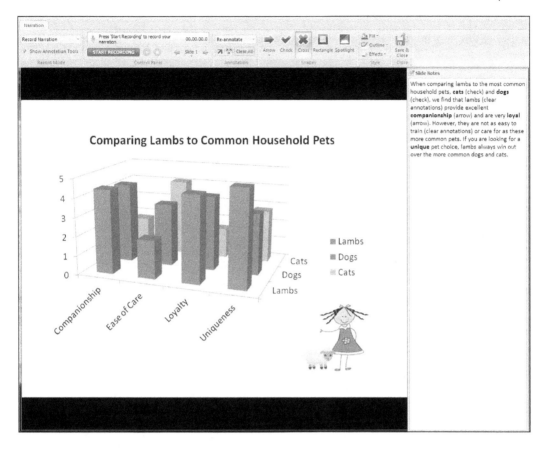

3
Preparing Your Player

In this chapter we will cover the following:

- ▶ Adding your company's logo
- ▶ Setting up a player template
- ▶ Setting up course defaults
- ▶ Attaching external resources to your course
- ▶ Previewing and publishing your course

Introduction

Now that we've created a course in Presenter, we need to prepare the player for it. The player is the skin for your Flash video presentation, which contains the controls, the information about the presenter, and additional supporting documentation for the presentation.

More than anything, the presentations created in Articulate are intended for use over the Internet as part of a training course. For this reason, it is both useful and necessary to add additional information and controls to the course. By doing so, you provide more complete control of the presentation to the viewer.

This also provides a way of adding some more information about your company, the presenter, and supporting documentation to the presentation without taking up the valuable "real estate" on the slides themselves.

While this part of the process can be done at any time, there are some steps that are best completed after creating the presentation itself. For this reason, we've put this chapter after *Chapter 2, Create Your Course with Presenter*. The idea is to completely create the presentation and then set up the presenter skin.

Adding your company's logo

Whether you're creating a training presentation or one for sales, you're probably going to want to take the opportunity to let people know about your company. In a regular PowerPoint presentation, this usually means putting your logo at the beginning and end of the presentation. Some people put it in a corner of the slides, taking up valuable "real estate", which is utilized for the message you are trying to present.

Articulate Presenter gives you the opportunity to provide your company's logo on every Flash video file without taking anything away from the slides. This is done by putting your logo in the sidebar. Articulate is able to do this because modern computer monitors have a "wide screen" format (aspect ratio of 16:9) while PowerPoint still operates in a standard format (aspect ratio of 4:3). The extra space in the monitor makes it easy to add the sidebar without reducing the size of the slide.

Getting ready

You'll need a presentation that you can work with, even if it is only one slide. You will also need an image that you can use as the logo:

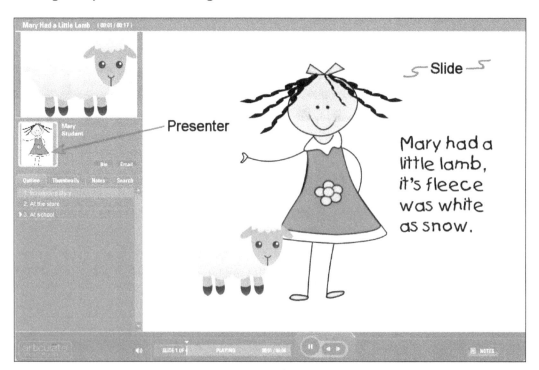

In this presentation I've used Mary's lamb as the logo. You can select any image that you want in the `.swf`, `.jpg`, `.png`, `.gif`, `.bmp`, `.emf`, and `.wmf` formats. The image must be 244 pixels wide, to fit the area on the presenter skin. Should you use a wider image, it will be reduced to that width. However, you are better off reducing the image before importing it into the library so that you do not make the file any bigger than necessary. This is especially important for presentations that will be distributed over the Internet.

Most paint-type programs allow the capability to resize images while maintaining their proportions. If you do not have a paint program on your computer, there are a number of freeware programs available online that you can use. One excellent one is Paint.NET, which you can download for free from `http://www.getpaint.net/download.html`.

How to do it...

Articulate Presenter works from a logo library, making it easy to keep a track of all the logos that you regularly use. So if you need to add the logo to the library, then tell Presenter which one you are going to use in your presentation. To add a logo perform the following steps:

1. The first step is to create a library of logos in the **Logos** tab of the **Presentation Options** dialog box. So we need to open the **Presentation Options** dialog box by clicking on the **Presentation Options** button on the **Articulate** ribbon.

2. The dialog box should open to the **Logos** tab. If it did not, click on that tab.

3. To add a logo to your library, click on the **Add...** button. A standard, Windows open file dialog box will appear, allowing you to search for and add your logo image:

4. Let's add two logos to the library. To add the second one, repeat the actions you performed in step 3. For now you can use any image.

5. To select your default logo, select the logo that you want to make the default, and click on the **Make Default** button located on the right-hand side of the list of logos. The logo which is selected as your default will have its text displayed in bold, indicating that it is the default.

6. You don't actually select the logo that you will be using in the presentation until you are at the point of publishing it. Clicking on the **Publish** button on the **Articulate** ribbon opens the **Publish** dialog box, as shown in the following screenshot:

7. The **Publish** dialog box has a drop-down menu for selecting the logo you wish to use from your library. Your default logo will show here unless you choose to change it.

How it works...

By creating a library of logos, you will be able to use the same logos over and over again, without having to search for them on every presentation. You can also select one of the logos in your library as your default logo, which will be shown if you don't select another. This library won't be published with the course. The only logo that will be published is the one you select. It will be added to the presenter skin.

On the screenshot of the **Presentation Options** dialog box from step 3 of this recipe, you can see that **Articulate Logo** is currently selected, making it blue. However, the **Mary's Lamb** logo is the default logo, which is obvious because it is bold.

The height of your logo is not limited by Articulate Presenter, although logos that are too tall will reduce the amount of space available for the navigation pane in the sidebar. To leave sufficient space for the navigation pane, the logo should be limited to the same maximum height.

You can also use an animated logo for your presentation's logo. To do so, it must be in the Shockwave (.swf) file format. If you are creating this Flash logo yourself, be sure that you select **action script 2 (AS2)** when you render the Flash video of your logo.

There's more...

If you need to use a logo that is not a part of your library, you can do so. This logo will need to be added to the presentation at the time of publishing.

To publish, click on the **Publish** button in the **Articulate** ribbon. This will open the **Publish** dialog box.

In the **Publish** dialog box, the button to the right-hand side of the logo's drop-down selection box with an ellipsis (three dots) on it opens the **Presentation Options** dialog box, allowing you to select the image that you need for your logo. Once the logo is selected, click on **OK** to add it to the presentation.

Unwanted images can be removed from the logo's library by clicking on the **Delete** button, located immediately below the **Add** button on the **Logos** tab of the **Presentation Options** dialog box.

Once the logo is selected, the only way that it can be seen is by publishing the presentation or previewing the presentation. Since you are already in the **Publish** dialog box, you only need to click on the **Publish** button to finish.

Setting up a player template

It is possible to set up the presentation in such a way that all the viewer sees is the slides themselves. That's what we did in *Chapter 1, Getting Started with Articulate Suite*, of this book. However, it is much more common to display the player with its sidebar, which shows who the presenter is and what is included in the e-learning course.

This presenter skin can be customized in a number of ways to meet your specific needs. So when we set up the player template, really what we are doing is setting up the skin. This provides you with the opportunity to control branding and maintain a consistent look to your theme.

Getting ready

You can perform this recipe at any point in the process of creating a presentation. The player template is separate from the presentation up until the time of publishing the presentation. So a player template can be created either at the beginning or at the end of creating the presentation.

How to do it...

Every presentation needs a template to work off . This is not the same as the PowerPoint template, which controls the appearance of the slides. This is the template for the presenter skin. To set up a player template, perform the following steps:

1. Open the **Player Templates** dialog box by clicking on the **Player Templates** button on the **Articulate** ribbon. As with many of the **Articulate** dialog boxes, this one has a series of tabs down the left-hand side, which give access to the various settings that can be changed on the player skin. The dialog box should open to the **Layout** tab, as shown in the following screenshot:

2. In the **Layout** tab, start with **View Modes**; check the **Standard view** checkbox and remove the checks from the **No sidebar view** and **Slide only view** checkboxes. Moving down the dialog box, check all of the checkboxes in the **Sidebar** and **Toolbar Menu** sections. This will cause your template to have the most options visible:

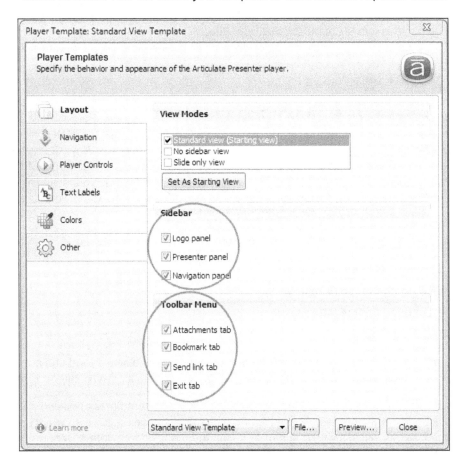

3. Select the **Navigation** tab. The first item is **User navigation**, which should show **Free – user can view slides in any order**. Click on all of the navigation tabs to check them, to allow the presenter to show all the viewing options. In the cases where it may not be advisable to give the viewer freedom to freely navigate to the presentation, options exist to restrict or eliminate the controls.

4. Select the **Text Labels** tab and verify that **Language** is set to **Use existing labels**.

5. Select the **Colors** tab. This allows you to change the player skin's colors. It does not affect the coloration of the slides. In the **Color scheme** drop-down list select **Blue Deep**. You should see that the colors change on the image in the center of the dialog box.

6. Select the **Other** tab. In the **Browser size** drop-down menu select **Resize browser to optimal size**. This will ensure that your presentation appears at its full size.

7. Now that all the settings are done, the changes need to be saved. At the bottom of the **Player Templates** dialog box is a pull-down menu that shows the various templates you currently have, both the built-in ones and those that you have created. Next to this menu is a button that says **File...**. Click on this button and then click on **Save As...**. When the new dialog box opens, fill in the name of your new template.

How it works...

Articulate comes with several standard templates designed to be compatible with the most common uses of the presentations made in Articulate Presenter. These templates are accessible from the player templates on the ribbon. At the bottom of the **Player Templates** dialog box, you will see a drop-down menu (arrow 1 in the screenshot under step 1 of the *How to do it...* section of this recipe) with the preinstalled templates and your saved templates. You can see that we have an added template called **Mary & her lamb**, which we created in *Chapter 1, Getting Started with Articulate Suite*.

The preloaded templates included in the Articulate Presenter are as follows:

- ▶ **Corporate Communications**
- ▶ **E-Learning Course (Single-level)**
- ▶ **E-Learning Course (Multi-level)**
- ▶ **Tradeshow Loop**

These names are fairly self-explanatory. The difference between a single-level and a multilevel e-learning course is whether it is branched or not. We will explain its details later on.

The preloaded templates are listed in blue while your personal templates are listed in black. If you select one of the standard templates and make any changes to it, when you try and save it, the program will ask you for a name, saving the modified template as a new one and thereby preserving the integrity of the preloaded templates.

All of the preloaded templates except **Tradeshow Loop** are very similar in appearance and have the sidebar. The **Tradeshow Loop** template does not have the sidebar but does have an orange launch button which the viewer has to press to start the presentation. Once a presentation that is created with this template is launched, it will continue to loop until stopped.

This dialog box provides much more flexibility for changing your player template. Each of the tabs in this dialog box allow you to make a number of very useful changes, as follows:

- ▶ **Layout**: This allows us to select whether or not the sidebar is visible, which items appear on the sidebar, and which tabs appear in the toolbar part of the sidebar.

- **Navigation**: This controls how much freedom the viewer is allowed in navigating through the presentation.

- **Player Controls**: This section is fairly straightforward, allowing you to select or deselect the controls that the viewer is able to use, including things such as volume, forward, backward, and pause controls, and a seekbar for finding a location in the presentation.

- **Text Labels**: Articulate Presenter comes with all the labels for the skin fully customizable. Upon opening this tab the labels will appear in standard American English. You can change this by selecting the **Language** tab, which will allow you to select from any of the other 11 languages (see the arrow in the screenshot):

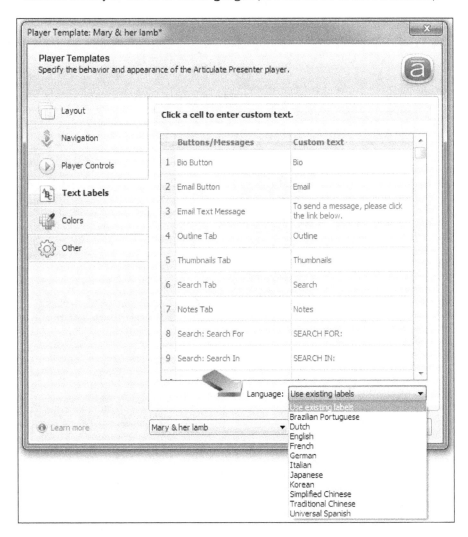

Additionally, you can customize any individual label by clicking on it in the **Custom Text** column and typing in a new name. This set of changes will be saved to your template, making it available to any presentation you create that uses the same template.

▶ **Colors**: Articulate Presenter allows the full customization of skin colors. There are 22 preinstalled color schemes, each of which can be further customized as you desire. In the following screenshot, the **Blue Deep** color scheme has been selected (arrow 1 in the screenshot):

▶ **Other**: This final tab allows for a selection of how your web browser displays the finalized Flash presentation. Specifically, it allows you to determine whether you want to change the browser size to match the presentation or the presentation size to match the browser. There are two drop-down menus, one for sizing the browser and the other for sizing the presentation.

There is also a checkbox for launching the presentation in a new browser window rather than creating a new tab on the existing window. If you select this, you are further allowed to select whether the browser controls are visible. Deselecting this can help ensure that the viewer is seeing your presentation rather than surfing the Internet:

When making these selections, keep in mind how your presentation will be viewed. In the case of using it for a trade show or in a training room, you may want to limit the viewer's ability to leave the presentation and browse other websites. However if your presentation is going to be on a website, not allowing the viewer to browse away from the presentation may annoy them, causing them to close the browser window. These are important questions, which can greatly affect the impact of your presentation.

The lower part of the dialog box deals with the slide titles shown in the sidebar of the presenter. **Display tooltip after** causes a tooltip-type balloon to open when your mouse rolls over a long slide title (one that is too long to display in its entirety), displaying the whole title. **Wrap title to a maximum of** allows the slide title to wrap the text that will take multiple lines to be displayed.

Once you have finished selecting all of your player template settings, you can preview how your presentation is going to look. There is a **Preview...** button at the bottom of the dialog box. Clicking on it causes Articulate PresenterTM to generate a preview of how your presentation will appear with the sidebar and skin. Please note that it does take a couple of minutes for the preview to generate, so be patient. Nevertheless, this is quicker than publishing your presentation in order to view it.

There's more...

The Flash video player is fully customizable, providing you with full control over what the viewer sees and what they are able to do with it.

Customizing the player navigation

After clicking on the **Navigation** tab, the upper section of the dialog box is titled **Navigation**. The first item is **User navigation is**. This allows you to select three levels of freedom for the user to navigate the presentation, as follows:

- **Locked – user cannot change slides**: This is for navigating backwards and skipping slides. It is useful if the course requires the users to listen to the audio and complete any interaction on the page. They are not allowed to advance, go back, or jump around until these items are completed.
- **Restricted – can only view current and prev slides**.
- **Free – user can view slides in any order**.

The next setting in this section of the dialog box is **Navigation Tabs**. This determines which of the tabs on the sidebar will be displayed. You can select any of them by clicking on the checkbox. You can also reorder them as you desire by selecting the tab and using the arrows on the right-hand side. Finally you can select which tab will be the starting tab when the presentation opens, by clicking on the **Set As Starting Tab** button below this list. Note that you must have the item that you want selected before clicking on this button.

The last selection in this area is a checkbox to determine whether the navigation scrolls to keep up with the point in the presentation. This is a nice way to allow the viewer to have an idea of where they are in the presentation.

The lower section of the dialog box deals with the appearance of the presentation in the **Navigation** section. Since it is displayed in the same manner as a directory tree, you can select when the "tree" expands to show the slides that are part of that level or branch.

A variety of player controls

On the **Player Controls** tab there are two sections named **Player Controls** and **Miscellaneous**. If there is no audio included in your course, you are going to want to either deselect the checkbox for **Volume Control** or leave it checked.

You can also select or deselect whether the skin shows things such as the "powered by" logo. See the following screenshot for the locations of the items that can be changed on this tab:

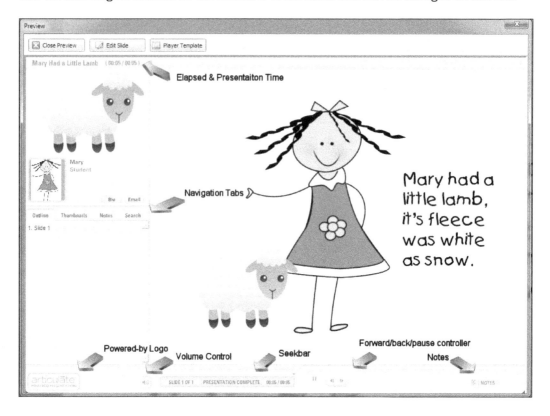

There are a few controls on this tab that could use some explanation. **Allow user to seek within seekbar** permits the user to select any point within the seekbar and go back to see the presentation again from that point. As you can see in the preceding screenshot, the seekbar is blue. This indicates that the whole presentation has been shown. By clicking on a point in the bar, the presentation would rewind to that point, showing the blue bar only at that point.

The **Loop presentation** setting causes the presentation to automatically start over again once it reaches its conclusion. This is ideal for use in an unattended sales kiosk, such as in a trade show.

Finally, the **Enable keyboard shortcuts** setting allows the use of Windows shortcuts but not Articulate shortcuts. Be aware of the environment in which your presentation will be shown before checking this checkbox.

Changing the language of the player labels

If you desire to create your own set of custom labels, perhaps for a language that is not currently installed in Articulate, you can do that as well. To do so, you will need a program that allows you to edit XML. If you don't have any other program to edit XML, you can do so in the Windows Notepad.

The easiest way to make a new text label set is to start with an existing set and modify it. You can find the label sets on your hard drive at **Program Files | Articulate | Presenter | Labels**. Open an existing file and use it as a template.

In the XML editor, you only need to locate the text that needs to be changed, which is shown outlined in red in the following screenshot. This screenshot is taken from the Spanish language text label set.

Be extremely careful when making your changes to only change the text labels themselves. The commands that are before and after the text labels, which are surrounded by brackets (< >), cannot be changed. If you accidentally eliminate one, the label will not work.

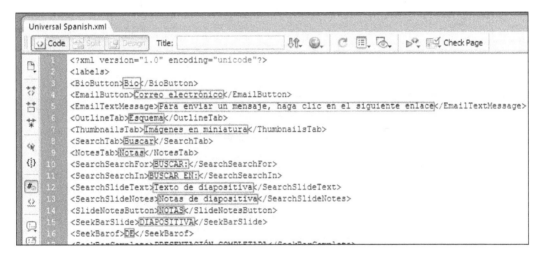

Be sure to save your new set as a new file using the **Save As...** option in your XML editor, so as to not lose the original language.

Your new language will show up in the pull-down menu the next time you open Articulate.

Full customization of color schemes

Although there are a number of built-in color schemes included in Presenter, there may not be the exact combination of colors that you need for your company's branding. Therefore, the creators of Articulate have given you the capability of totally customizing the player colors. To customize the color schemes, perform the following steps:

1. By clicking on the **Edit Color Schemes...** button on the **Colors** Tab, a dialog box opens allowing you full customization of every element's color in the skin. This dialog box will provide a mockup of the presentation in the skin, with the slide area replaced by the colorizer.

2. Within the colorizer, there are a number of checkboxes and radio buttons for individual items. Click on individual items and then select the color to apply to them from the color selector in the middle of the colorizer, as shown in the following screenshot:

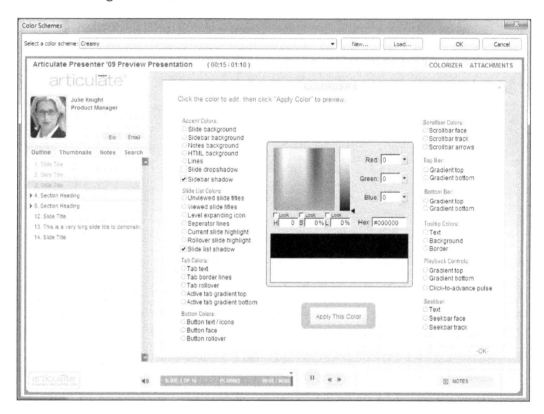

3. To see how your new color looks for that item, click on the **Apply This Color** button.

4. Your new color scheme can be saved by clicking on the **New...** button at the top of the dialog box.

Setting up course defaults

In *Chapter 1, Getting Started with Articulate Suite*, we discussed how to create the individual slides for your presentation, and in the previous recipe, we discussed how to set up a template for the player. Now we will discuss the presentation defaults, that is to say, how Articulate Presenter cycles through the slides. Everything we are going to do is from the following two buttons on the **Articulate** ribbon:

- The **Presentation Options** button
- The **Slide Properties** button

Both of these buttons can be found in the **Tools** section of the ribbon, as shown in the following screenshot:

Getting ready

In order to set up the course defaults, it is necessary to have a presentation to set them up in. While the first part of the process that is done in the **Presentation Options** dialog box isn't slide specific, the second part of the process that uses the **Slide Properties** dialog box is. So you'll need to open up an existing presentation or create a simple one that you can use.

How to do it...

We need to set up the presentation options first, as some of the slide properties will require information about what we are going to set up in the **Presentation Options** dialog box. To set up the course defaults, perform the following steps:

1. To open the **Presentation Options** dialog box, click on the **Presentation Options** button on the **Articulate** ribbon. You will find a number of tabs along the left-hand side, each of which deals with different aspects of the presentation.

The first tab presented is the **Logos** tab. We have already explained how to add a logo so we will not repeat that here.

2. Clicking on the **Presenters** tab allows you to add additional people to your library of presenters. The presenter also shows up on the sidebar below **Logos**.

3. Selecting the presenter here will indicate the person who is presenting at the beginning of the presentation. You can change the presenters throughout the presentation. This is especially useful if you have multiple presenters involved in an e-learning session, each of whom has responsibility for a different section of the presentation. If you don't change the presenter in the middle of the presentation, the same presenter will stay on the sidebar throughout the presentation:

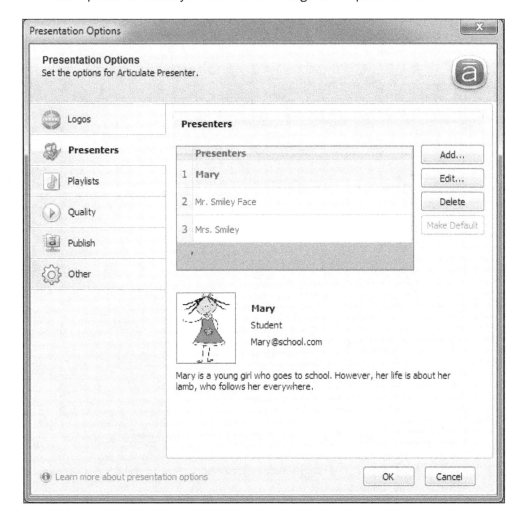

4. Clicking on the **Add...** button opens a dialog box for inputting the presenter's biographical information.

5. This dialog box allows you to enter the presenter's name, title, e-mail, and a brief bio. In the lower part of the dialog box, a photo of the presenter is added.

6. Clicking on the **Browse...** button in the dialog box opens a standard, Windows open file dialog box for selecting the photo:

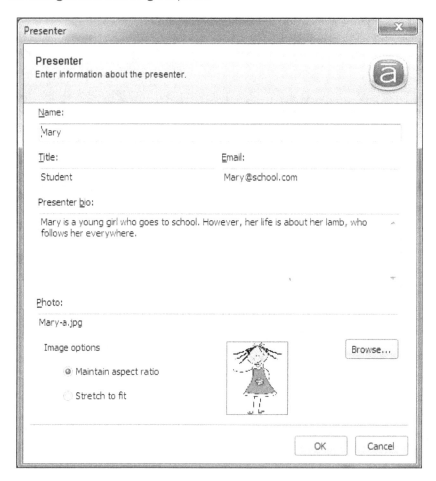

7. Once you finish adding the biographical information, click on the **OK** button to return to the previous dialog box.

8. Like the **Logos** tab, you can select any of the presenters in your library to be your starting presenter by clicking on the **Make Default** button. The presenter's photo and biographical information will appear at the bottom of the **Presentation Options** dialog box.

9. There are two preset quality levels available in the **Quality** tab, plus the ability to select your own settings. The two presets are **Optimize for Web Delivery** and **Optimize for CD-ROM Delivery**. Select **Optimize for Web Delivery**.

10. Click on the **Publish** tab. The top item mentioned is the delay time for slides without audio or animations. If your slide has narration or animation, the slide won't change until after those have finished playing. However if your slide doesn't have any narration or animation, this allows you to determine how long it will be before the slide advances. The default is **5** seconds, which is ample time, except in cases where there is a lot of text for the viewer to read. In the cases where you are going through a number of photos, such as a slide show, you may want to reduce this to 2 or 3 seconds.

   In the cases where you don't have any animation, just a series of images, such as our "Mary Had a Little Lamb" example, you can run this as slow as 1 frame per second without degrading the quality of the presentation in any way.

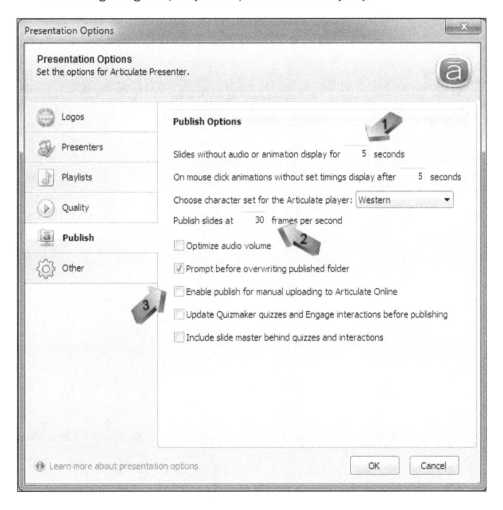

11. Select the **Other** tab. In the **Recording** section of the dialog box, there are two important settings. The first is **Show notes print on narration window**. Clicking on this allows you to see your notes while you are recording the audio.

    The second important checkbox in this section is **Record narration for one slide at a time**. This allows you to control your recordings better. Professional recording studios prefer to do it in this way because it provides the greatest opportunity to eliminate errors:

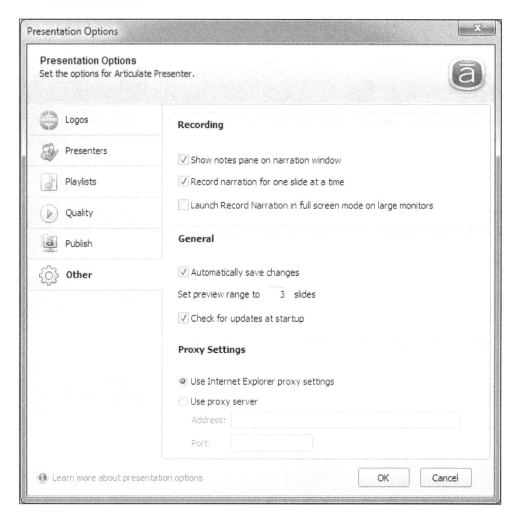

12. This concludes everything necessary for setting up the presentation options. From here we're going to move on to slide properties, which will allow us to apply some of these settings to individual slides in the presentation. Click on the **OK** button to close the dialog box.

13. Click on the **Slide Properties** button on the **Articulate** ribbon to open up the **Slide Properties** dialog box. This dialog box doesn't have any tabs, but presents us with a chart of the various slides in the presentation along with a number of settings that can be selected for each of the slides. Since some of these settings are dependent upon what we did with the presentation options, it is important to set those options up before attempting to set up the slide properties:

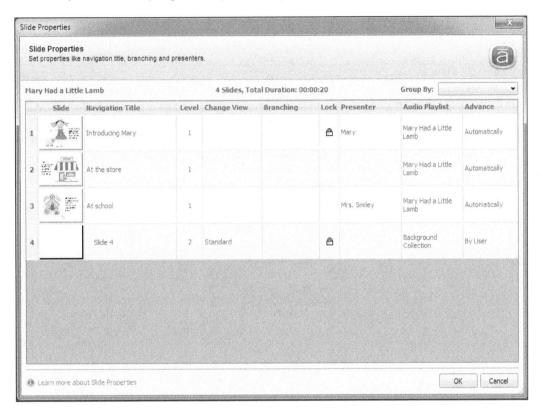

14. You will need to set the various options in this table's columns for each slide in your presentation. This will tell Articulate how to handle those options for each slide, when it renders your Flash video presentation.

15. Click on a thumbnail in the **Slide** column that here will enlarge it, allowing you to see it better.

16. The default for the **Navigation Title** column is "Slide x", where x is the number of that slide in the column. Since these navigation titles will be shown in the sidebar allowing the viewer to select the individual slides that they want to see again, it's important to have navigation titles that refer to what is on the slide. Clicking on the individual cell in the table allows you to erase the existing navigation title and type in your own.

17. The **Lock** column stops the player controls from working for the duration of that slide, preventing the viewer from navigating off that slide. They are still allowed on-slide navigation and access to any hyperlinks. Clicking on this cell puts an image of a padlock into the cell, indicating that it is locked:

18. You can select a presenter for your presentation. In the **Player Templates** dialog box, we created a library of presenters and selected one as our default. If we don't select anything in this column, then that default presenter will be used. Change the presenter in one of the slides by clicking on the cell in the table. A drop-down list of all the presenters in the library will appear allowing you to select the presenter for that slide, as shown in the following screenshot:

19. You do not have to select the presenter for each slide. Once you select a presenter, it will be displayed until you indicate a change. If you look at the screenshot at the beginning of this section, you will see that **Mary** was selected as the presenter for the first slide and **Mrs. Smiley** was selected for the third slide. Since nobody is selected for the second slide, Mary will continue to be displayed until the third slide is displayed.

20. The audio playlist that will be used needs to be selected for each slide. The default setting is silence if we have not selected a playlist. Like **Presenter**, clicking on the **Audio Playlist** cell opens a drop-down list allowing you to select from the various playlists that you have saved in the library. If you select the same playlist across multiple slides, it will continue to play, even by looping (if so selected), until you select a different playlist:

Presenter	Audio Playlist	Advance
Mary	Mary Had a Littl ▼	Automatically
	Background Collectic	Automatically
	Mary Had a Little Lai	

21. The final column in our table is **Advance**, which controls how the presenter advances from that slide to the next one. There are only two options for this—**Automatically** and **By User**. With the automatic setting, the slide will advance once the narration and animations are finished, or at the time for automatic advance that you set up in the **Publish** tab of the **Presentation Options** dialog box. The **By User** option requires a mouse click by the viewer to go to the next slide.

How it works...

The **Quality** tab in the **Presentation Options** dialog box shows up not only here in Presenter but also in the other Articulate suite products.

The web delivery option is great for use over a broadband connection. However, if you are expecting your viewers to be using a dial-up service, they probably won't be able to view your presentation well. The CD-ROM option has a higher quality image, especially for video. Although called CD-ROM Delivery, this is the same option you would want to use if you are planning on showing the presentation directly from your computer.

The third option, **Custom**, is for establishing your own settings where the disk space might be at a premium or where your viewers might be watching the presentation through a dial-up Internet connection. Selecting **Lossless** gives you the highest image quality, essentially the same as you would have if you had selected **Optimize for CD-ROM Delivery**. The **Lossy** setting allows you to reduce the file size by sacrificing the quality of the image delivered. A recommended setting for **Quality factor** is **75**, which still provides good image quality on a screen resolution of 600 x 800 pixels. However, corporate America is currently using a screen resolution of 1280 x 960 pixels.

If you are preparing the presentation for a dial-up connection, you'll need to drop this setting to 35-40. At this level, the image won't be as clear. However, it will be able to be transmitted through a modem.

Resize factor deals with how well your image can maintain its quality if it is resized. A setting of **2** is normal. Lowering the number also lowers the quality:

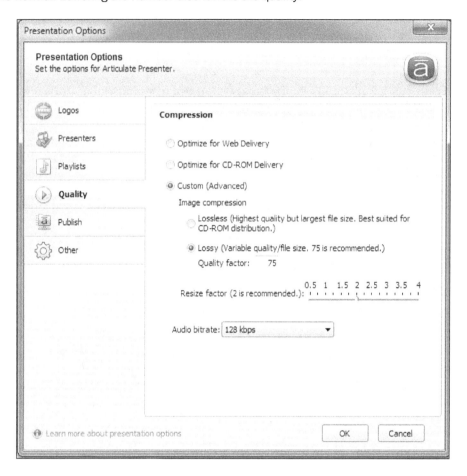

The last setting here is **Audio bitrate**. The pull-down menu allows you to select from 16 to 160 kbps (kilobits per second). The lower the number, the lower your audio quality is going to be. While this may not be much of a problem with narration only, if you have any music, the lower bitrates will distort the music. For comparison, CDs are recorded at 128 kbps, an FM radio station transmits at 80-96 kbps, and an AM radio station transmits at 48-56 kbps. The recommended setting is 64 kbps to provide a good balance between size and quality.

There's more...

Not every presentation is the same, nor is every person who is trying to create a presentation trying to do the same thing. Therefore, you might need to add some special settings to your course.

Setting outline level

Articulate Presenter allows you to group your slides in an outline. This can be useful for organizing long presentations, having the sections as level one and individual slides within that section as level two, with supporting information as level three, and so on.

To change the level, click on the number contained in this box of the chart. You will only be able to go down one level from the previous slide and not skip over levels. If you look at the screenshot of the dialog box, you'll see that **Slide 4** has been changed to level **2**. The navigation title is indented to indicate this, as shown in the following screenshot:

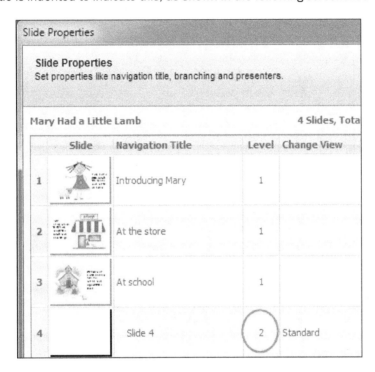

When your slides appear in the navigation pane on the sidebar, they will follow the outline format with the lower-level slides being indented. Depending upon the settings you chose in the **Levels** section of the **Navigation** tab in the **Player Templates** dialog box, the lower levels of the slides will either not show up till the viewer gets to that section of the dialog box, or not expand at all, or allow the viewers to decide when they want to see it.

Changing the template used for viewing the presentation

When we were setting up the player template, we selected a view for the presentation. This view is the default that will be used throughout the presentation. The three options we have for the **Change View** column are as follows:

▸ **Standard**: This is for showing everything in the viewer

- **No sidebar**: This is for eliminating the sidebar and showing only the slide and the controls (located below the slide)
- **Slide only**: This is for eliminating both the sidebar and the controls

If we do nothing here, then whatever we selected for the template will remain throughout the presentation.

If we want to change the view for part of the presentation, we could do so here. One time that we might want to do this is for video. During the video, we might want to eliminate the sidebar allowing the video more room. Another instance would be for an introduction slide where we don't want the navigation or sidebar to be visible.

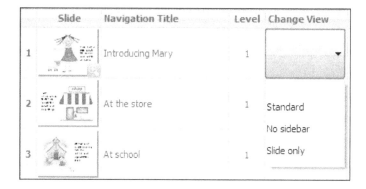

Clicking on this cell in the table opens a drop-down menu where we can make our selection between the three view modes.

Hiding slides in the presentation navigation pane

By right-clicking on any slide number in the **Slide Properties** dialog box, you open up a context-sensitive menu that includes the various settings in the chart. It also includes a selection for **Hide In Navigation Panel**. Selecting this would keep that slide's name from appearing in the list of slides in the **Navigation** panel on the sidebar:

You may want to hide certain slides from the navigation pane if they contain elements of an animation that must be seen as a group. In such a case, you'd only want to show the first slide in the group so that the viewer can see the whole animation. Another time you may want to use this is if you are branching your presentation and want the branch slides to remain hidden.

Attaching external resources to your course

It can be very useful to allow your viewers access to external resources that are not part of the presentation. These can consist of anything, such as instructions for using the presentation, reference information, supporting documentation for claims and statistics presented, websites that have further information, or interactive activities that support the material in the presentation.

Regardless of the reason for these external resources, in most cases, they have to be listed separately and usually aren't accessible from within the presentation or training course. Recognizing this problem, Articulate includes the capability to provide a list of resources right in the player.

Please note that these are not in your presentation but rather are accessed from the **ATTACHMENTS** tab, which is located in the toolbar menu at the top of the player above your slides, as shown in the following screenshot:

Getting ready

To complete this recipe, you'll need a presentation with at least one slide. Adding some graphics to the slide will help you see how it will look when inserted into the player.

How to do it...

The attachments that we are adding are not part of the presentation that was created in PowerPoint, but rather are accessed through the skin. Therefore we need to add them through Articulate. Perform the following steps to do so:

1. In order to use the **ATTACHMENTS** tab, you must have it selected in the player template. Open the **Player Templates** dialog box from the **Articulate** ribbon.

2. This dialog box should open with the **Layout** tab that was selected. In the **Toolbar Menu** section, select the checkbox for **Attachments tab**. You can also find the controls to select the other tabs that are shown in the preceding screenshot in the same area:

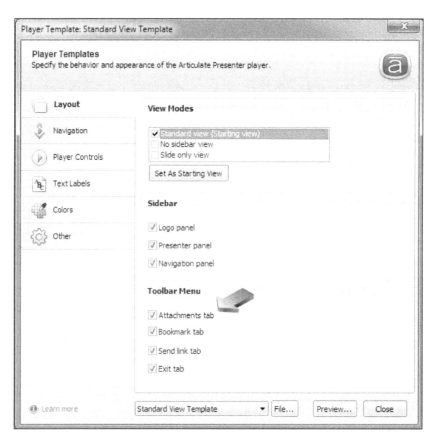

The **Attachments** dialog box is accessed through the **Attachments** button located in the **Insert** section of the **Articulate** ribbon. The dialog box has a column table that is prenumbered and that allows you to add the resources you want the viewer to have available as attachments to the presentation:

3. In the **Title** column, type in the name of the resource that you would like to attach. You want to make sure that this name is something descriptive, which will help the viewer understand what the resource is and how it will help them. While you can use longer titles, only about 30 characters will be visible:

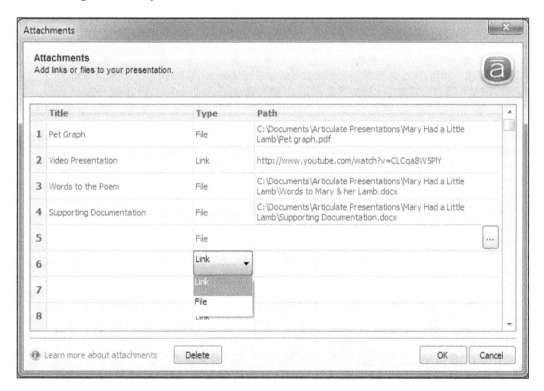

4. In the **Type** column, you can select between **File** and **Link**. Selecting a cell in this column provides a drop-down menu where you can make your selection.

5. The **Path** column is where you would put the URL of the Internet resources or the location of any of the files on your computer. To find the files on your computer, you can select the ellipsis button (**...**) located on the right edge of the column.

Remember that these attachments aren't actually being added to the slides of your presentation but rather to the player itself, so you will not see any changes by adding them until you either preview or publish your presentation.

How it works...

Literally anything that can be put on a computer can be added to your presentation as an attachment (links, `.doc` files, `.pdf` files, videos, and images). However, you need to be sure that these resources will be accessible to your presentation when it is shown. In other words, if you are attaching files on your computer as resources, you will need to make sure that if the presentation is moved to another computer, uploaded to the Internet, or put on a CD, that all of these resources are copied along with the presentation files.

The easiest way to ensure that everything is copied together is to create an `attachments` subfolder in the folder that houses your presentation. Even if those documents reside elsewhere on your computer, copy them to that file, using those copies as the ones that you link to from the **Attachments** dialog box.

Of course, this problem doesn't exist for the online resources that you include in the **ATTACHMENTS** tab. In that case, the URL of the web page will function regardless of where your presentation is:

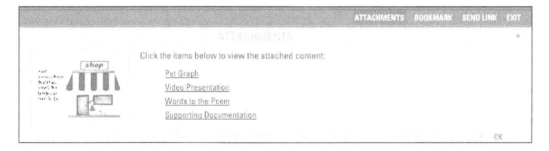

You can add up to a maximum of 50 attachments to any presentation. When you click on the **ATTACHMENTS** tab in the presenter, a list of all your attachments will open. Only the names will be visible and not the URLs or file locations.

Previewing and publishing your course

Once you have finished your course, you'll obviously want to do something with it. This is one of the places where Articulate Presenter differs from PowerPoint. With PowerPoint you simply save your presentation and show it to your audience. However, Articulate will convert your presentation to a Flash video. Doing so requires publishing it, allowing the program to create the video files.

Publishing takes a bit of time, so before actually publishing your presentation, it can save you time if you preview it. This allows you to view how the presentation will be published so that you can ensure that everything is going to look the way you want it to.

Getting ready

If you've been using the same presentation to try out all these recipes, you've already got something to use for previewing and publishing. If not, open any PowerPoint or Articulate presentation that you have on your computer.

How to do it...

There is no way of seeing exactly how the presentation will look without allowing Articulate to publish it. The difference between publishing and previewing is that in previewing, permanent files aren't created. For previewing and publishing your course, perform the following steps:

1. Both the **Publish** and **Preview** buttons are located in the **Publish** section of the **Articulate** ribbon. When you click on the **Publish** button, it gives you three options as follows:

    ❑ **Preview This Slide**

    ❑ **Preview Next 3 Slides**

    ❑ **Preview Range of Slides**

    You can see the same options in the following screenshot:

2. Choose the **Preview Range of Slides** option, which will cause a dialog box to open. In it you can select the range of slides that you wish the program to create a preview of. The dialog box will provide thumbnails so that you can better identify the slides you want to preview, as shown in the following screenshot:

3. Once you have selected your range of slides, click on the **Preview...** button. It will take some time for the program to create your preview. It is doing everything necessary for publishing the Flash video except creating the permanent files. A dialog box will appear, showing you the progress of the preparation process.

4. The preview is a fully functional version of your presentation, including your player settings and attachments. The only things that won't function are any hyperlinks and web objects that you have placed in your slides. However, those hyperlinks will function in the published version of the presentation:

5. There are three buttons on the top bar of the **Preview** window above the toolbar menu. The first of these is for closing the preview (it does the same thing as clicking on the red "X" in the upper-right corner of the window). The second one is for editing the slide. Clicking on this button will return you to PowerPoint for editing the slide. If you want to return to the preview after making changes, you will need to use the **Preview** button on the ribbon. The third button allows you to make changes to the player template. Clicking on it opens the **Player Templates** dialog box. This allows you to select a different player template, change the logo being used, or change the presenter, as shown in the following screenshot:

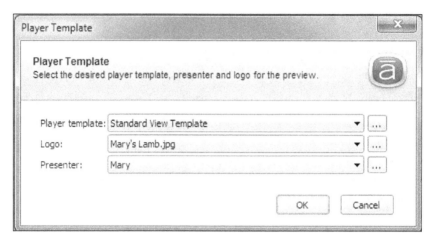

6. Now that you have previewed and approved your presentation, let's publish it. Articulate is capable of publishing in a variety of different forms for a variety of different uses. Clicking on the **Publish** button on the right edge of the **Articulate** ribbon opens the **Publish** dialog box. The various publishing formats are shown as tabs along the left-hand side.

7. Select the **WEB** tab on the left-hand side of the dialog box. This is the most common way of publishing Articulate presentations and distributing them via the Internet.

8. When publishing to the Web, one of the biggest concerns is the file size. Even with most people using broadband connections, there are still limitations to how fast they can receive information. Those who are still on dial-up connections have even bigger limitations on file size and throughput.

9. The **WEB** tab allows you to select the folder where you would like your presentation to be stored on your computer, for uploading it to the Web later. If you are unsure of the location, simply click on the ellipsis button (**...**) to the right-hand side of the textbox, which will open a standard Windows browse dialog box for you to find the folder:

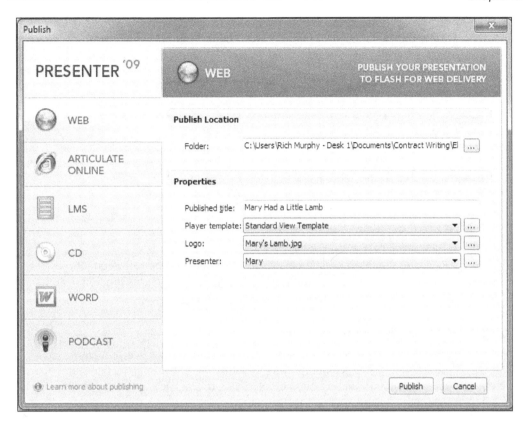

10. In addition to selecting the location that your presentation will be published to, you also need to give it a title. This title will be used when the folder is created for your presentation.

11. You also have the option of changing the player template, logo, and presenter. If you do not make any changes at this time, your defaults will be used.

How it works...

Although the default option for the number of slides shown in the preview is three slides, you can change that number if you want to. To do so, open the **Presentation Options** dialog box and go to the **Other** tab. In the **General** section of the tab, you will see a statement that says, **Set preview to 3 slides**. The number **3** will be in a textbox; you can replace this with whatever number you want.

Although you may be publishing presentations for use on the Web, you won't actually be publishing them to the Web; you will be publishing them to your hard drive. Afterwards, you or your web manager will need to publish them to the Web using an FTP program. The only exception to this is if you are using Articulate Online. Articulate allows you to publish directly into your account on Articulate Online.

When publishing your presentation, keep in mind that you will be creating more than one file. Actually, the program will create a folder with the presentation name, which contains two subfolders and a `player.html` file. You can rename the `player.html` file as desired, but you cannot rename the subfolders or the files that they contain. All of these are a part of the presentation and must be included in any uploads, or if you move the presentation to another location on your computer.

There's more...

Although publishing to the Internet on an existing website is the most common form of distributing Articulate presentations, there are other methods. Articulate Presenter works very well with online **learning management systems** (**LMSs**) as well.

Publishing to Articulate Online

Articulate Online is Articulate's own LMS. It is a paid subscription service that allows you to create online learning courses for corporate, educational, or commercial use. You need to create an account with Articulate Online before using this service, as shown in the following screenshot:

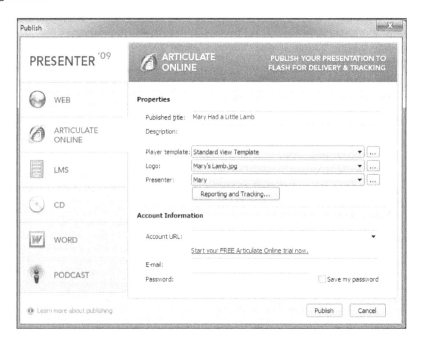

In addition to the settings used for creating a presentation for use on the Web, the **ARTICULATE ONLINE** tab has a place for you to input your account information and logon password. This is because the program will automatically connect to the Articulate Online website and upload your course once it has finished creating the files.

There are two other pieces of information that you can provide for your presentation when publishing to Articulate Online. You are allowed to provide a course description, which will need to be typed into the textbox below the title. You will also need to select the manner in which you want Articulate Online to track and report students' progress and grades. This is done by selecting the **Reporting and Tracking...** button on the dialog box.

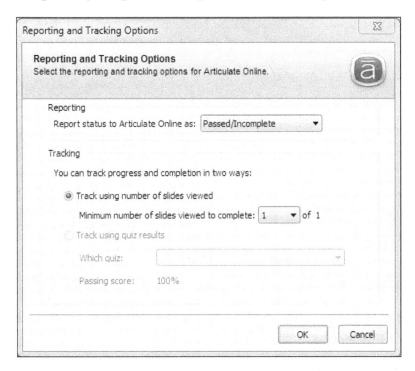

The new dialog box that opens allows you a number of options for tracking learner progress. The first of these is the reporting status of the learner's progress. There are four different "either/or" options in a drop-down menu, as follows:

- **Passed/Incomplete**
- **Passed/Failed**
- **Completed/Incomplete**
- **Completed/Failed**

Below this is the area for deciding how you would like the progress to be tracked. There are essentially two options, based on the number of slides viewed or the quiz results. The quiz results option can only be used in cases where you have quizzes included in the presentation; otherwise this area is grayed out, as was shown in the preceding screenshot.

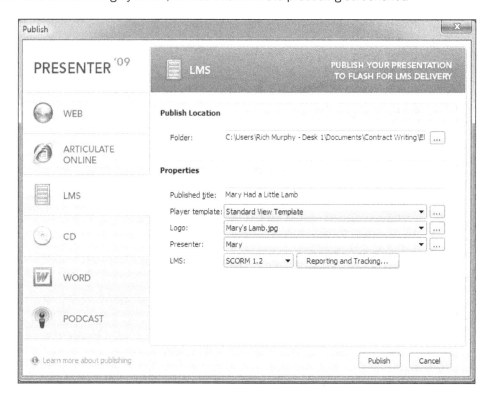

The passing score for a quiz is something that you set up when you create the quiz. Although it is shown in this dialog box, you cannot change it from here.

Publishing to an online LMS

This tab is used when you are creating presentations to use with other online LMS services. Most of the information contained on this tab is the same as those previously mentioned, with the exception of the LMS format. There are three formats supported by Articulate, as follows:

> ▸ **SCORM 1.2**: Shareable Content Object Reference Model
> ▸ **SCORM 2004**: Further refinable by selecting the second or third edition
> ▸ **AICC**: Aviation Industry CBT Committee

There is also the **Reporting and Tracking...** button on this tab for opening the **Reporting and Tracking Options** dialog box, just as there is with the **ARTICULATE ONLINE** tab. However, the dialog box is more complicated and changes to match the selected LMS format.

Publishing to a CD

Other than the Internet, CDs are the most common means for the distribution of presentations. The **CD** tab performs almost identically to the **WEB** tab. The major difference is that the formatting of any video for CD mode doesn't concern itself with file size as it does with web mode. It is assumed that the video will fit on the CD.

Publishing to Microsoft Word

This provides you with the ability of producing note sheets for use by the presenter or for use as handouts. The output is similar to the print options provided in PowerPoint. The major difference is that the presentation is output to a document in the Microsoft Word format and not directly to the printer.

There are two different formats you can output the presentation to. You can select this difference with the Notes version.

The storyboard version provides thumbnail images of the slides along with the notes and information about each slide.

The **Notes** section does not supply the thumbnails or slide information but just the title and notes.

This is the storyboard version. Note that this is the most complete version that can be printed, as shown in the following screenshot:

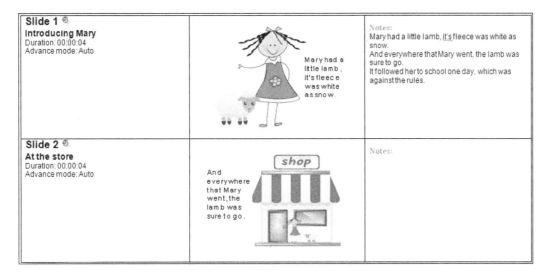

Please note that the Word output is created in the Word 97-2003 format. While this should not cause any problem if you open it in a newer version of Word, it might change the formatting slightly.

Publishing a podcast

The **PODCAST** tab allows you to produce an audio-only copy of your presentation. This would then either be used alone or in conjunction with the printed slides that can be created in the **WORD** tab. This will produce a `.mp3` file for distribution.

For a podcast, there is additional information that should be included. Since podcasts are intended to be predominantly for music, it is common to include the artist and album as a part of the audio file's header. In the case of a class, this could be the presenter's name and training course series.

On this tab, you also have the capability to select the audio quality that you would like the program to produce your podcast in. The default is high quality, which is 128 kbps (kilobits per second). This is equivalent to the quality level of a music CD. By comparison, FM radio is 80-96 kbps and AM radio is 48-56 kbps.

4
Creating Assessments and Courses with Quizmaker

In this chapter we will cover:

- ▶ Setting up a quiz template
- ▶ Adding a basic graded question
- ▶ Adding a basic survey question
- ▶ Creating a hotspot question
- ▶ Customizing the question and answer
- ▶ Adding images to a slide
- ▶ Changing a slide's background color and theme
- ▶ Creating slide masters
- ▶ Adding audio to a slide
- ▶ Adding video

Introduction

Articulate Quizmaker is an application for creating Flash-based quizzes, assessments, and even training courses. Unlike Presenter, Quizmaker is a standalone application, which can be used either independently or in conjunction with Presenter. This product does not require PowerPoint or Presenter to function. However, quizzes created in Quizmaker can be easily imported into Presenter.

Although the focus of this program is to create quizzes and assessments, it is possible to create entire courses purely in Quizmaker, without the use of Presenter or any of the other programs in the Articulate suite.

To open Quizmaker, you need to click on the icon on your desktop or program menu. This will open the program and a welcome dialog box. The box that will appear gives you three basic choices, as follows:

- ▸ **Create a new quiz**
- ▸ **New from quiz template**
- ▸ **Open a recent quiz**

If you have quiz templates installed or have used the program recently, the names of those files will show up under the heading of that program. Both the **New from quiz template** and **Open a recent quiz** headings have a **Browse** button just below them, to allow you to find any items, as shown in the following screenshot:

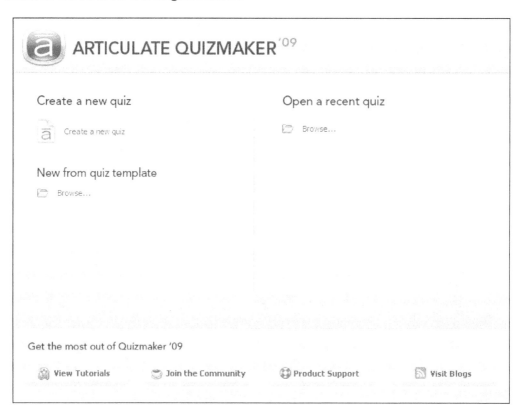

Since you're just starting out with Quizmaker, you aren't going to see any recent quizzes or quiz templates listed. However, if colleagues or coworkers have created quizzes or templates in Quizmaker, you'll be able to access those through the **Browse** button if you have access to the same files; see your network administrator if you do not.

To begin with a new quiz, you'll need to click on the **Create a new quiz** button. This will open a dialog box, asking you whether you want to create a graded quiz or a survey. Both have similar question types, but the graded quiz is set to score and show the user the results. You have to start with one or the other but can combine the two, making some questions a quiz and others a survey.

 Graded quizzes are tallied so that the learner receives a grade for their work. Survey quizzes are all tallied together and provided to the owner of the survey.

The main difference that this selection makes is when it comes to the results of a quiz. If you create a graded quiz, you have the capability of providing pass/fail feedback to the user. This capability does not exist with a survey quiz; instead, the survey results are tallied.

Setting up a quiz template

To set up any type of quiz, we're going to need a template. Just like in Presenter, this template is for the program's "skin" and not for the content of the quiz or course itself.

Getting ready

You'll need to open the Articulate Quizmaker program. Once open, select **Create a new quiz** from the opening screen. Since we are going to create a quiz template, select the tab in the dialog box that says **Graded Quiz** and click on the **OK** button.

Quizmaker's main screen will open, showing you the **Home** ribbon that says **No questions** in the list of questions, as shown in the following screenshot:

How to do it...

Any quiz template you create can be used with multiple quizzes; this is one of the ways that you can create the "branding" of a teaching series or of your company. To set up a quiz template, perform the following steps:

1. On the **Home** ribbon click on the **Player Templates** button. This will open the **Player Template Manager** dialog box, as shown in the following screenshot:

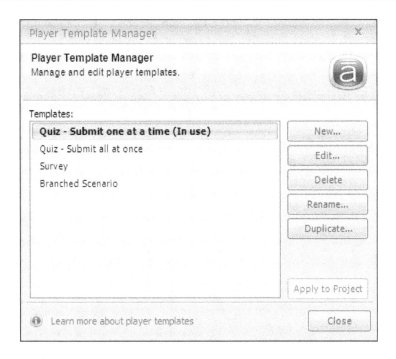

2. There are four types of player templates that are listed. We're going to select the first one, called **Quiz – Submit one at a time**. Then click on the **Edit...** button to modify this template.

3. The **Player Template Builder** dialog box will open, allowing you to make changes to this template. Click on the **Navigation** tab.

4. We're going to select the first radio button that says **Submit one question at a time**. This allows the program to provide feedback to the user for every question. If we had chosen **Submit all at once**, the feedback would not have been given until the quiz was completed.

5. Let's also check the checkbox in the **Resume** section that says **Prompt to resume on quiz restart**. This will allow the user to restart at the point where they left off rather than starting over again. Since we are not using a **learning management system** (**LMS**), we're not going to check that checkbox:

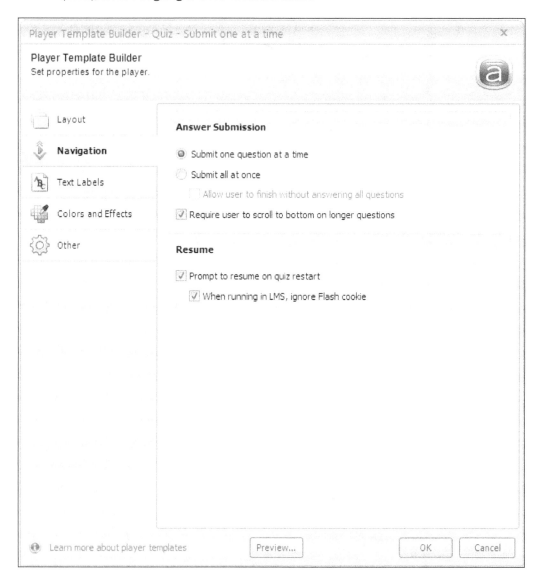

6. Click on the **Text Labels** tab. We're going to make sure that the language selected in the drop-down menu in the lower-right corner of the screen says **English**.

7. Now we're going to change the color of the skin by clicking on the **Colors and Effects** tab. At the top of the dialog box, there is a drop-down menu where we can select from the preinstalled color schemes. Let's select **Green Forest** from the list.

8. We also want to alter the fonts and effects in the lower part of the dialog box. Select **Disable** from the **Sound effects** drop-down menu. The very last item we can change is labeled **Display likert scale tooltips after**. Insert 100 in this textbox. This is in milliseconds, which are thousandths of a second. So 100 milliseconds is one-tenth of a second.

A **likert scale** is a method of grading that is commonly used for surveys. It provides a series of five to ten graded responses where the respondents can select their reaction to a question. Normally, the lower end of the scale is rated as "strongly disagree" and the higher end is "strongly agree". The respondent is therefore able to select their degree of agreement or disagreement with the statement that has been made.

9. Select the **Other** tab. This allows us to determine how the user's Internet browser will act when the quiz is launched. To prevent causing the browser to resize, possibly causing problems for other things they are working on, we're going to check the checkbox for **Launch player in new window**.

When opening the quiz in a new window, the user's browser cannot have an active pop-up blocker present or it will prevent the quiz from operating properly. An instructional note should be given to the users informing them of this potential problem.

10. Now that we have all of the settings made for our template, let's check them by clicking on the **Preview...** button at the bottom of the dialog box. This will show us how the skin will look along with colors, fonts, and controls.

11. We still need to save our new template. To do so click on the **OK** button. This will open a dialog box asking us to give our new template a name. Type in the name and click on the **OK** button.

How it works...

The settings we just created are global settings, which will be used throughout the quiz. Since we have saved them as a template, the same group of settings can be used over and over again without having to recreate them for each quiz. All that needs to be done is to click on the **Player Template** button on the ribbon and select the template we want to use in the **Player Template Manager** dialog box.

The **Layout** tab, which we didn't change, allows you to make some global decisions about how the quiz looks. Specifically, the choices made here affect the amount of information that is given to the learner as they take the quiz.

Adding a basic graded question

A quiz consists of a number of questions. These need to be added individually. While a combination of question types can be added, we're going to start with multiple-choice questions.

Getting ready

You'll need Articulate Quizmaker open on your computer. You are going to add a graded question, so you'll want to select **Graded Quiz** in the **New Quiz** dialog box and click on the **OK** button. When the quiz is created, it will not have any questions in it.

How to do it...

All questions are added in basically the same manner, regardless of the question type. The only difference is the format of the question. We're going to be adding a multiple-choice question, but the same basic procedure applies to all the other types of questions. Perform the following steps to add a basic graded question:

1. Even though you've selected for this to be a graded quiz, you'll still need to select that for every question. Click on **graded** in the **Question 1** box under **Question Group 1**, as shown in the following screenshot:

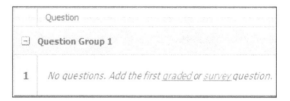

2. The dialog box should open with the **Multiple Choice** tab selected. If it is not selected, select it and click on the **OK** button. This will open a dialog box for entering your question and the possible answers.

3. Type the question into the textbox that is labeled **Enter the Question**. In addition to the question, you should use this area to enter any instructions to the learner. Many people don't realize that they need to click on the **Submit** button after selecting the answer, so a typical instruction might read `Select your answer to the question and click on the "Submit" button`.

4. Type the possible answers into the **Choice** boxes in the **ENTER THE CHOICES** section of the dialog box. You can enter up to 10 possible answers.

5. Select the correct answer in the column that says **Correct**. When you select it, the radio button should fill with a 3D blue dot.

6. At the bottom of the dialog box there is the **SET FEEDBACK AND BRANCHING** section. To change the existing feedback, click on the existing answer and type in your own, as shown in the following screenshot:

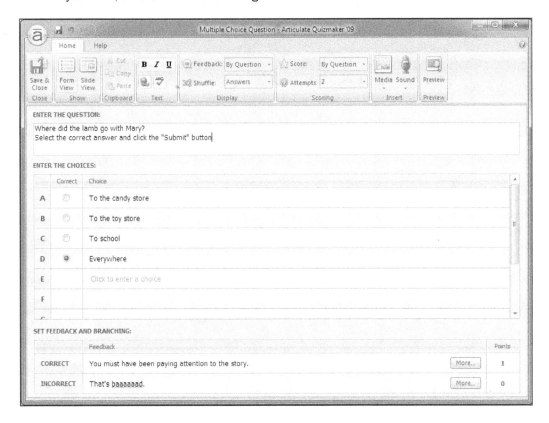

7. To the right-hand side of the **Feedback** column is a column labeled **Points**. The default for this is 10 points per question. Click on the number **10** and replace it with **1** to change the number of points that the question is worth.

8. In the **Scoring** section of the ribbon, you can set the number of attempts in which the learner has to try and get the right answer. The default is **1**. Click on the down arrow to view the drop-down list and select **2**.

9. Preview how the question will appear in the quiz by clicking on the **Preview** button in the ribbon. It will take the program a minute to generate the preview, as it is applying the settings from the template we created in the *Setting up a quiz template* recipe of this chapter.

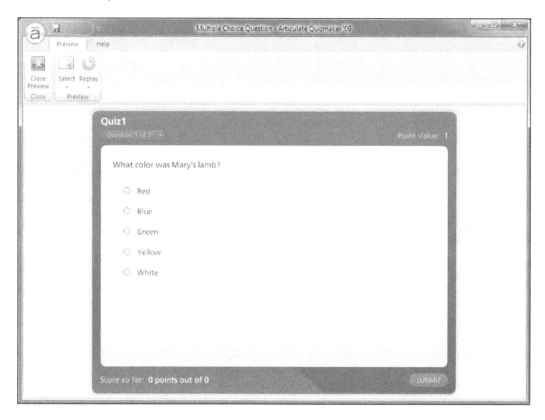

10. Once you are sure that your question is correct, click on the **Close Preview** button to return to the dialog box where you created the question.

11. Before leaving this dialog box, the question must be saved. This is done by clicking on the **Save & Close** button on the ribbon.

How it works...

Quizmaker is highly automated, making the process of adding questions easy. From the simple information that we've added, it is able to create the slide for the question and its underlying code to make the grading portion of Quizmaker function.

There are a number of question formats that can be used in Quizmaker. The type of question is selected in the **New Graded Question** dialog box, the one that appeared when you clicked on **graded** in step 1:

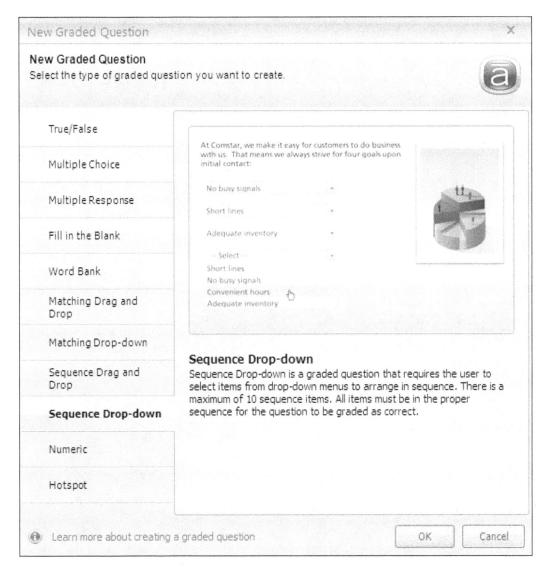

As you can see from the preceding screenshot, there are 11 different question types that Quizmaker can work with. For many of these, the actual details of how many responses there are, is left up to the creator.

These question formats are mostly the same formats that have been used by instructors for years. The major difference is that Quizmaker allows them to be used interactively on a computer. This ability captures the current generation much better, providing a more complete engagement in the learning activity.

There's more...

A lot can be done with the questions that are added into Quizmaker. Not only can different types of questions be used, but the questions can also be modified in a number of different ways.

Once your question is entered into the quiz, you can return to it, to edit it, by double-clicking on the question in the list.

Additional questions can be added by clicking on the **Graded Question** or **Survey Question** button in the **Insert** section of the ribbon. This opens the same dialog box for creating questions that we just used. When you save the question, it will be added to the list.

Adding hyperlinks to question text

At times, it might be useful to allow the viewer to be able to see additional information along with the question. One way to do this is to provide a hyperlink in the question so that they can reference that information. Perform the following steps to do so:

1. Highlight the text that you want to add a hyperlink to and select the **Insert Hyperlink** button in the **Text** portion of the ribbon. This will open the **Insert Hyperlink** dialog box for entering the hyperlink, as shown in the following screenshot:

2. Type the web address to the resource that you want hyperlinked into the **Address** textbox. To make it easier, you can copy the URL from the web page and paste it into this box. To paste it, right-click on the box and select **Paste** from the context-sensitive menu that appears.

3. Test your hyperlink by clicking on the **Test** button to the right-hand side of the hyperlink.

4. Select the radio button for **Display in new browser window** and click on **Save** to add your hyperlink to the slide.

See also

▸ The *Creating a hotspot question* recipe

Adding a basic survey question

Quizmaker includes the ability to use both graded and survey questions. We've already added a graded question, so now we're going to add a survey question. The difference is that the survey questions are not graded, rather the results are tallied as survey data.

Getting ready

You'll need Quizmaker open for this recipe. You can either use the quiz you already started in the last recipe or create a new one.

How to do it...

Adding a survey question is very similar to adding a graded question. The major difference between the two is the manner in which they are graded. Graded questions provide a grade to the learner while survey questions tally everyone's results together. To add a basic survey question, perform the following steps:

1. If you're starting with a new quiz, click on **Survey** in the box for the first question. If you are adding to your already existing quiz, click on the **Survey Question** button in the **Insert** section of the ribbon, as shown in the following screenshot:

2. The **New Survey Question** dialog box should open with the **Likert Scale** tab that is open. If it does not, click on that tab and then click on the **OK** button.

3. The dialog box that opens for entering your question and statements looks very much like the one we used for entering the graded question. The major difference is that the **Feedback** area only allows one answer instead of two, nor is there any way of scoring the question.

4. Enter the statement that you want the reader to respond to in the **ENTER THE INSTRUCTIONS** textbox, as follows:

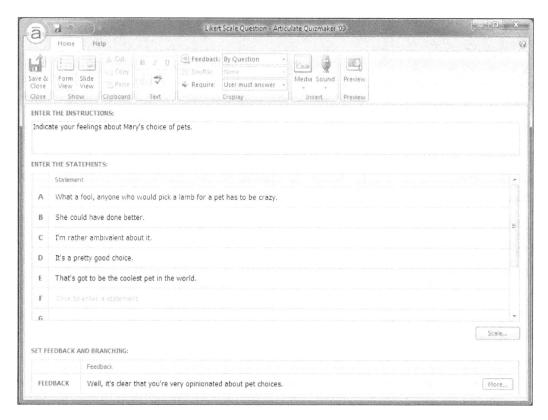

5. Enter your answers in the lines contained in the **ENTER THE STATEMENTS** table. Each box needs to contain a separate statement, which would be the person's reaction to the instruction statements. You can enter up to 10 different statements. These are typically ranked from **Strongly Disagree** at the top of the list to **Strongly Agree** at the bottom of the list.

6. Click on the **Scale...** button. A dialog box will open, allowing you to check your answers against how they will be graded. This list will automatically be adjusted with the number of statements that you have provided. Verify that your answers are in agreement with the list.

7. You can change any grades in this scale by clicking on them and typing in a new label. Once finished, click on the **OK** button to return to the **Question** dialog box.

8. At the bottom of the **Question** dialog box it says **SET FEEDBACK AND BRANCHING**. Type in your feedback for the person answering the question.

9. In the **Display** section of the ribbon is a setting for **Require**. Click on the drop-down menu and set this to **User must answer**.

10. Click on the **Preview** button in the ribbon to see how your question will look in the Flash video. Since the program is generating the preview with the skin that we created in the *Setting up a quiz template* recipe of this chapter, it will take a minute to appear.

11. When done checking the preview, click on the **Close Preview** button on the ribbon to return to the **Question** dialog box.

12. Click on the **Save & Close** button on the ribbon to save your question.

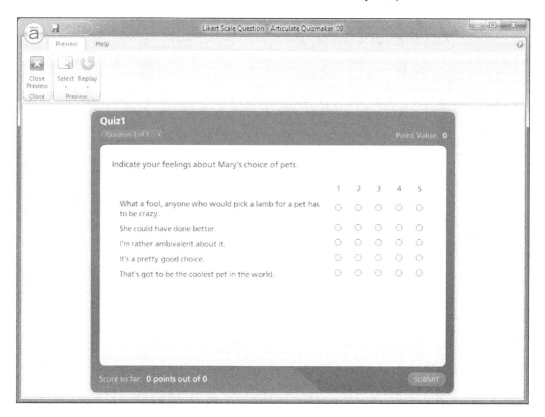

How it works...

The Likert scale is a common way of asking questions, as it recognizes that not everything is black and white. Using this method provides a way for people to grade their response, providing a "gray" answer instead of just "yes" or "no." While Likert scales can be created with any number of levels, the most common size is of five possible choices per question.

There are nine different types of survey questions that Quizmaker can generate. Selection of the question type is made from the **New Survey Question** dialog box, which opens when you click on the **Survey Question** button in the ribbon. While there are differences in how each of them are created, the process is similar. The program will automatically set up your information in the correct question format.

These different methods are also similar to the various question types for graded quizzes. We won't be covering them as survey questions; we will be covering only the graded questions.

There's more...

At times, it can be useful to change a survey even after beginning to use it. Quizmaker allows the possibility of editing your survey questions at any time.

Modifying questions

You can edit a survey question even after you've saved it, by double-clicking on the question in the main Quizmaker screen. This will open the **Question** dialog box, which allows you to make any changes that are required.

Creating a hotspot question

Most of the question types are added and modified in pretty much the same way as the multiple-choice questions are. The exception to this is the hotspot question, which is a graphical question.

Getting ready

As we're adding a question, you can work on either a blank quiz or one that you already have. The hotspot questions don't exist in survey quizzes, so you'll need a graded quiz.

How to do it...

The hotspot questions are graphical questions where the viewer selects a part of the image or one image out of a bunch of images as the correct answer. The part that he/she is going to select is the "hotspot". Perform the following steps to create a hotspot question:

1. Click on the **Graded Question** button in the ribbon to open up the **New Question** dialog box. **Hotspot** is the bottom tab in the dialog box. Select it and click on the **OK** button.

2. For hotspot questions, it's best to work from **Form View**. The first thing you'll need to do is type in the question in the textbox that says **ENTER THE QUESTION**. Be sure to include a brief statement of instruction, telling them to select the answer from the image.

3. Click on the **Choose Image...** button to add an image to your question. This will open a Windows open file dialog box for you to select your image from.

4. Click on the **Add Hotspot** button. This will open up a drop-down menu where you can choose from **Add Oval**, **Add Rectangle**, or **Add Freeform**. Let's select **Add Freeform** from the list, as shown in the following screenshot:

5. Adding a freeform hotspot requires selecting points around the outside edge of the shape that you want to make the hotspot. It's much like connecting the dots, but the only difference is that you're just creating the dots. When you get back to the beginning and close the shape, it will fill up with a green color with handles appearing around it:

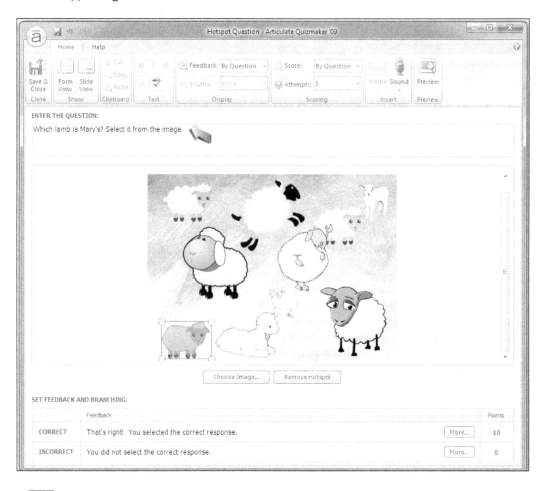

6. To further format the question switch to **Slide View**. This will allow the addition of more images and picture effects, such as frames and shadows.

7. Click on **Save & Close** in the ribbon to return to the Quizmaker main screen.

How it works...

We used the freeform hotspot in this recipe because it is the hardest to work with. The oval and rectangle hotspots are created by clicking on one corner and dragging it to the opposite corner. Once created, they can be resized or moved with the use of the handles on the edges of the hotspot image.

Although the hotspot appears in green on your work view, it will not appear the same in the quiz; it will be transparent. The learner will need to click on the hotspot to get the answer correct. Clicking anywhere else on the image will cause a wrong answer, with associated feedback.

There's more...

Hotspots can be added in **Slide View** as well. The **Add Hotspot** button is located in the **Insert** ribbon. Multiple images can also be added in **Slide View**, but only one hotspot can exist per slide.

Using hotspots with video

Although hotspots are intended to primarily work with pictures, they can be used with videos as well. Doing so requires a video where the object to be selected remains in one place, or where the object to be selected becomes visible when the video ends. Perform the following steps:

1. To add a video, hotspot requires being in **Slide View**.

2. Select the video by clicking on the **Flash Movie** button in the **Insert** ribbon. Remember that the video format must be `.swf`, `.flv`, or `.mp4`. Place and size the video on the slide as needed.

3. Add the hotspot to the video in the same way as it is done with an image. If the object moves slightly in the video frame, you may want to make the hotspot slightly larger than the object.

See also

▸   The *Adding video* recipe

Customizing the question and answer

Up to now we've allowed Quizmaker to format the question according to its built-in template. However, that may not always work out well and may not meet our needs. So Quizmaker includes a way to totally customize the format of any question.

Getting ready

We're going to need Quizmaker open and a new graded question selected. We're going to create another multiple-choice question.

How to do it...

There are two ways of looking at the questions in Quizmaker, namely **Form View**, which we've been using, and **Slide View**, which is where we have the capability of making more formatting changes. Perform the following steps to customize the questions and answers:

1. After clicking on the **Graded Question** button in the ribbon, click on the **Sequence Drag and Drop** tab of the **New Graded Question** dialog box. Then click on the **OK** button.

2. Since we want to make a custom layout, we don't want to use **Form View** of the question dialog box; so we're going to click on the **Slide View** button on the ribbon.

3. The dialog box will change to show a blank slide. In this mode, adding information is much like adding it in PowerPoint. Type your question in the box that says **Click to add question**.

4. Let's resize the question box by grabbing the handle on the right edge of the outline. Pull the box towards the left-hand side. The text will automatically reformat, wrapping onto the next line, and the textbox will become longer in order to accommodate the additional line of text.

5. Now let's move the question halfway down the left-hand side of the slide. To do so, move your mouse cursor over the outline of the box. The cursor will change from an arrow to a four-headed arrow. Click-and-hold your left mouse button and move the textbox. Notice that a guideline appears along the left-hand side of the box so that you can move it straight down, without moving it from side to side:

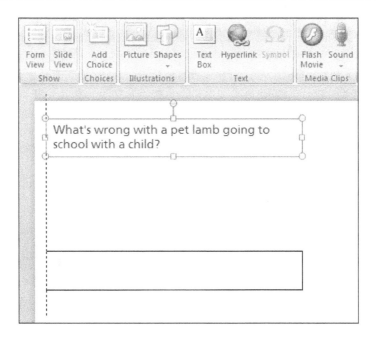

6. We now need to add our choices for the answer. To do so, switch to the **Insert** tab on the ribbon and click on the **Add Choice** button. You should see a box appear with a radio button in it.

7. Enter a choice into the textbox.

8. The location and size of this box is based upon the slide template, but is not adequate for this purpose. Let's resize it to only be on the right-hand side of the slide. This is going to require two steps. First, we grab the handle on the middle portion on the right-hand side of the textbox with our mouse cursor, and drag it to the left-hand side.

 To resize these boxes, you must shrink them from the right-hand side. Although it is possible to shrink them from the left-hand side, this will make the choice we've just added disappear.

9. Looking at the choice we have just created, we'll see that its textbox is outlined by a solid line. We'll also see a dashed line on the slide with the choice textbox in the upper-left corner. This is the template location for the choices. Although the textbox for that answer has been resized, any further choices that are added will be of the same width as the dashed box. To eliminate this problem, click on the dashed line, which will make it change to a solid line.

10. Grab the right handle on the box and use it to resize the width of the box to match the width of the choice you have added. Then click and hold the cursor on the edge of the box to drag it to the right-hand side of the slide.

11. Click on **Add Choice** to add another choice to your slide. Enter the choice into the new textbox.

12. The choices aren't filling up the whole side of the slide. To space them out farther, grab the edge of the bottommost choice with your mouse cursor and drag it down to the bottom of the dashed box. Do the same with any other choices, spacing them evenly.

13. Click on the radio button next to the correct choice. A blue spot should appear in it, as shown in the following screenshot:

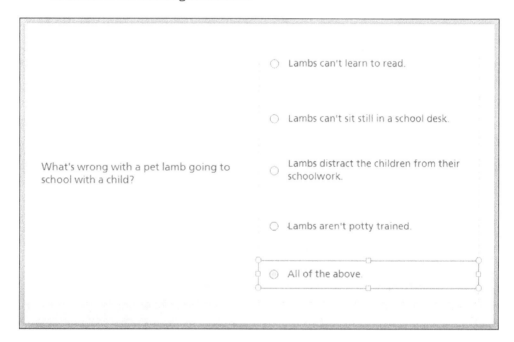

How it works...

We have just accomplished the same thing that we did when we entered the information in **Form View**. However, by working in **Slide View** we were able to customize the layout of the information, making it fit to our needs better.

There's more...

You can use both views together to make the process easier. The question and choices can be entered in **Form View**, and then you can switch over to **Slide View** to adjust the formatting.

See also

▸ The *Adding images to a slide* recipe

Adding images to a slide

In today's highly visual world, where websites are often more about the graphics than the content and movies are filled with special effects, it's important to provide visual stimulation in presentations of any kind. Graphics can add a lot to a presentation, quiz, or even a survey.

At times, these graphics might be diagrams necessary to explain a concept, while at other times, they might be pictures that illustrate a point; in other instances, graphics may be added just to help us maintain learner interest. Regardless of the reason, the ability to add graphics is an important part of creating any presentation.

Even though Quizmaker was created for quizzes and surveys, it has the capability of being used for entire presentations. Therefore, it also includes the ability to add and manipulate images.

Getting ready

You'll need a slide that already has a question on it. If you have saved the questions that you made in the **Adding a Basic Graded question** section, it would be perfect for this. If not, quickly create a slide with any question and answers.

How to do it...

Images can be added in either **Form View** or **Slide View**. We're going to add them in **Slide View** as that provides more options for formatting. To add images to a slide, perform the following steps:

1. Open the slide that you are going to add the image to. It will open in **Form View**. Switch over to **Slide View** by clicking on the **Slide View** button on the ribbon.

2. Select the **Insert** tab to change the ribbon.

3. In the **Illustrations** section of the ribbon, click on the **Picture** button. This will open up a standard Windows open file dialog box for you to search in and select your image. Once you have found the image and clicked on it, click on the **Open** button.

4. The image will appear in the center of the slide. Resize it by clicking on any of the handles and dragging. If you click on one of the corner handles, its size will change proportionally.

5. Click on the green handle in order to rotate the image, as shown in the following screenshot:

6. Click-and-hold anywhere on the image and move it to a new location by dragging-and-dropping it.

7. When you click on the image, the ribbon changes to the **Format** tab. This allows the customization of the image in a number of ways. Click on one of the thumbnails in the **Picture Styles** section to add a frame to the image, as shown in the following screenshot:

8. In the **Picture Styles** section of the ribbon, select the **Picture Effects** button. This will open a dropbox with the various types of effects that are available. Select **Reflection** to open the fly-out menu that shows the various types of reflections that are available. Select a reflection to add to the image, as shown in the following screenshot:

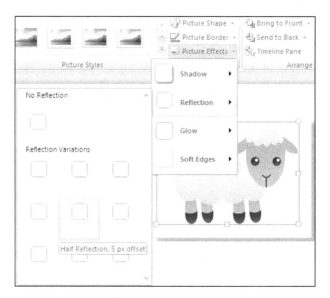

9. In the **Size** section of the **Home** tab of the ribbon is a button called **Zoom Picture**. This does not affect the picture as you see it on the slide. It adds a button to the picture that allows the viewer to enlarge the picture to its original size. This can be especially useful for situations where you have a diagram on the slide that the learner needs to refer to, in order to answer the question.

10. To add additional images to the slide, repeat steps 3 through 9.

11. Click on the **Preview** button on the ribbon in order to see the quiz, as it will only be presented once the Flash video is created. This will add the skin that we created in the *Setting up a quiz template* recipe of this chapter.

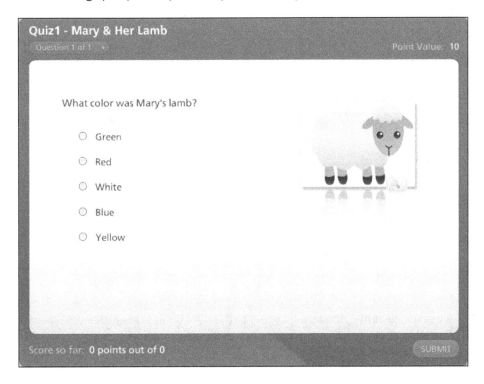

How it works...

Articulate Quizmaker has many of the same built-in picture effects that PowerPoint does. The tabs and ribbons have intentionally been made similar to what you are used to in PowerPoint, in order to shorten the learning curve. You can also change the brightness and contrast of your image, recolor it, or crop it to best fit your needs.

There's more...

Although we added our image in **Slide View**, it can also be added in **Form View**. If you are trying to create a quiz in a hurry and are not as concerned about the layout of the quiz, this is a fast and easy way to add images.

Adding images in Form View

It is also possible to add images to the slide in **Form View**, although only one image can be added per slide. This image will be added in the default image location as determined by the slide master. Perform the following steps:

1. From **Form View** of the question, click on the **Media** button in the **Insert** section of the ribbon. This will open a fly-out menu where you can select **Picture...**, as shown in the following screenshot:

2. Once you click on **Picture...**, a standard Windows file locator dialog box will appear, where you can select the picture that you want to add to that slide. Once you have selected it, click on the **Open** button in the dialog box.

3. A thumbnail of the picture will appear to the right-hand side of the question in the **Question** dialog box. If you would like to make any modifications to this picture, you need to switch over to **Slide View**.

See also

▶ The *Animating images and objects* recipe in *Chapter 2, Create Your Course with Presenter*

Changing a slide's background color and theme

A good presentation needs to be visually attractive. That isn't just for the sake of looking good, but also to help us capture and maintain the viewer's attention. The attention to detail that makes a presentation look good also makes it look more professional, which helps convince the viewer that the creator knows what they are talking about.

For those who are used to working with PowerPoint, style themes are a familiar concept. They are used to help create the "branding" of the presentation or a series of presentations, in order to identify with the company or the series of teachings that are being created.

Themes in Quizmaker are worked on very much like they are in PowerPoint. However, the themes that come with Quizmaker are not the same themes that are used in PowerPoint, nor can a PowerPoint theme be imported into Quizmaker.

Getting ready

You'll need a slide with a question on it to work with. If you have saved your previous work, you can open one of those to work with. If not, create a quick quiz or survey question. Switch over to **Slide View** as the **Design** tab doesn't exist in **Form View**.

How to do it...

There are already a number of built-in themes in Quizmaker. These are readily accessed or can be modified to meet your personal needs. Perform the following steps:

1. Click on the **Design** tab of the ribbon to access the **Themes** section, as shown in the following screenshot:

2. To select a theme, click on its thumbnail in the **Themes** section of the ribbon. There are more themes than what are visible. To access the rest of the themes, use the scroll bar at the right end of the thumbnails; or you can use the down arrow button at the bottom of the scroll bar to open a dropbox that shows all the installed themes. Hovering over the thumbnail opens a tool tip with the name of that theme. Select **Satin**.

3. Each theme has a particular color scheme and font set that has been chosen by the designer to work with. The color scheme will affect the background, lettering, and shapes that are used on the slides. Click on the **Colors** button to the right of the theme thumbnails to open the color themes dropbox. Select the **Flow** color scheme, as shown in the following screenshot:

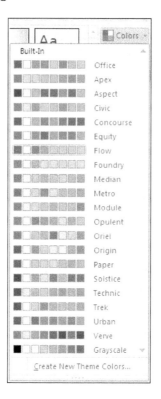

4. The backgrounds for the standard themes can also be varied. To do so, click on the **Background Styles** button in the **Background** section of the ribbon. This opens a dropbox with a number of different styles, as follows:

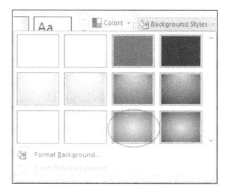

5. Select the style circled in the preceding screenshot. This particular style will put a highlight in the middle of the background without changing the background's color or design. Selecting the one to its right would change the background to be monochromatic while maintaining the design.

6. As we have made a number of changes to the theme, let's save it as a new theme. To do so, click on the down arrow next to the theme thumbnails to open the theme dropbox. Then click on **Save Current Theme...**. This opens a standard Windows **Save As...** dialog box where you can save the theme. The new themes will show up in the dropbox as follows:

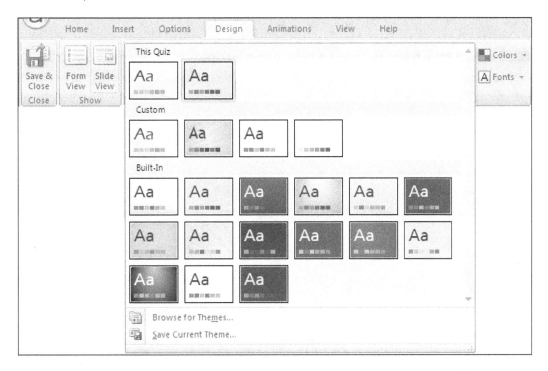

As you can see in the preceding screenshot, two areas have been added to the top of the dropbox. The **This Quiz** section has all the themes that are used in this presentation, regardless of whether they are custom or not. The **Custom** section contains all of the custom themes that you have created.

How it works...

Although the themes are not common to Windows, the color schemes and font sets are. These are the same sets that are found in Microsoft Office. So if you are accustomed to using a particular color scheme or font set for corporate branding, then you can use the same ones in your Quizmaker presentation.

Although the color scheme affects the background color for the preinstalled themes, it will not do so if you create your own theme using a photo for a background.

The font sets consist of two fonts, one used for headings and the other used for text. This is the maximum number of fonts that it is recommended to use on one page or slide. Adding additional fonts doesn't make the slides more impressive; it causes confusion for the reader.

There's more...

What we've done so far is pretty basic. However, themes can be changed quite extensively showing your personal style or your company's branding.

Modifying the background style even more

What we did when we set the background style was to apply a semi-transparent gradient fill to the background we selected. This was a "radial fill". However we can do much more than that. Let's play with it a bit by performing the following steps:

1. In the **Background Styles** drop-down menu from the ribbon select **Format Background**. This opens a dialog box for modifying the background.

2. Select the **Gradient Fill** radio button from the three options at the top of the dialog box.

3. In the dialog box next to **Angle**, type in the number 45 (signifying 45 degrees):

Original "Satin" Theme   With Radial Gradient Fill   With Linear Gradient Fill at 45 degrees

Applying textures to the background fill

It is also possible to use a picture to create a textured background. There are 35 textures included as part of the Articulate package. You can also find a large number of texture images on the Internet, which you can use as a background. To apply textures to the background fill, perform the following steps:

1. Access the texture option in the same way that you applied the gradient fill, by clicking on **Format Background** in the **Background Styles** drop-down menu.

2. Click on the radio button next to **Picture or texture fill** at the top of the dialog box.

3. Click on the button next to **Texture** to open the fly-out menu that shows the available textures. Select a texture by clicking on the thumbnail.

4. If you can't find a texture that suits your needs, click on the **File** button to select a texture from your computer. This will open a standard Windows open file dialog box so that you can find the texture graphic.

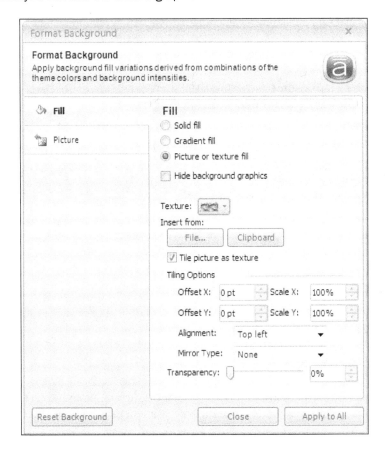

Using a picture as a background

The commercially available and free background templates, which you can find on the Internet for PowerPoint, use pictures for their background. These are not tiled pictures, as with a texture, but rather full-size images that are used. Quizmaker also provides this capability. For using a picture as a background, perform the following steps:

1. Access the **Format Background** dialog box in the same way that you did for adding the gradient fill to your slide's background. Click on the **File** button in order to find the picture that you want to use as your background.

Ideally, the pictures used for backgrounds should be 720 x 540 pixels. If you download pictures from the Internet that are advertised as being backgrounds, they will generally be this size. If you are using another picture, you will need to resize it to this size in a paint program.

2. Once the picture is imported to the slide, it may need to be modified. Select the **Picture** tab in the **Format Background** dialog box.

3. On this tab, you can adjust the color, brightness, contrast, and transparency of the picture that you are using as a background.

Creating slide masters

The style you use in your presentations is an important part of creating your company's branding, helping people to recognize your work or the work of your company. While you may not be the only one using a particular background or image, people will start to identify it with your company.

To help with this branding, Quizmaker allows you to create your own style either by modifying an existing theme or starting one from scratch. However, this applies just to style elements. You can't add in placeholders for textboxes or images.

Getting ready

You can create a slide master either from an existing Quizmaker file or by starting with a new quiz. You'll need Quizmaker and a question to be open, to be able to enter into the slide master.

How to do it...

To access the slide master you have to be in **Slide View**. It doesn't matter which question you are using as this will apply to all the questions in a quiz. Perform the following steps:

1. From **Slide View** click on the **Show** tab. On the ribbon, find and click on the **Slide Master** button. This will open the **Slide Master** screen and ribbon.

2. From the ribbon select the **Themes** button. Select the **stripes** theme. You can modify the background style in the same way that it was modified in the previous recipe.

3. Add another master by clicking on the **Insert Slide Master** button on the ribbon.

4. Rename the new slide master by clicking on the **Rename** button in the **Edit Master** section of the ribbon. Each slide master can have its own individual name:

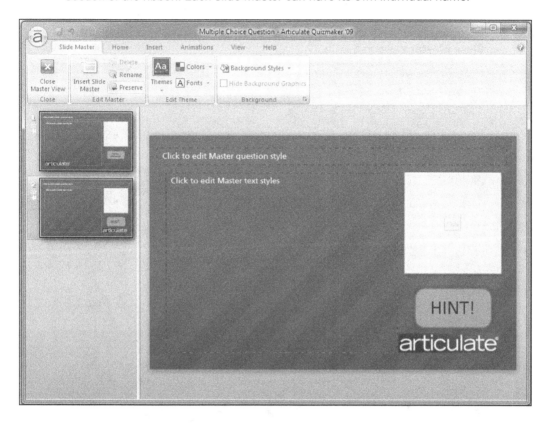

5. Add a picture by clicking on the **Insert** tab and then click on the **Picture** button. A Windows open file dialog box will open for you to select your picture from. You can move the picture wherever you want on the slide master.

6. You can modify the picture using any of the formatting options that you used when adding an image to the slide. The **Format** tab on the ribbon becomes available when the picture is selected:

7. You can modify the attributes associated with the picture placeholder in the slide master, in the same way that you can in a slide. These attributes will apply to the images in all the slides.

8. Add a shape to the slide master by clicking on the **Shapes** button on the **Insert** ribbon. The **Shapes** dropbox will open, allowing you to select a shape. These shapes can be modified to the same way that they are in the slides.

9. When you have completed adding shapes to the slide master, click on **Close Master View** on the ribbon:

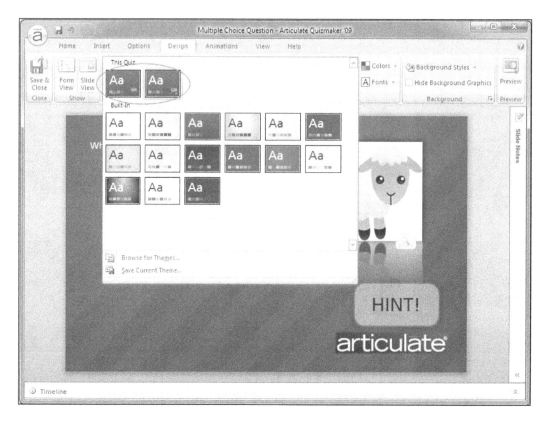

10. To apply the master to a slide you need to be in **Slide View**. From there, go to the **Design** tab on the ribbon, and use the **Themes** section of the ribbon to select the slide masters you created. When you click on the arrow for the themes drop-down menu, they will appear in the first row.

How it works...

Slide masters in Quizmaker are more limited than they are in PowerPoint. While you can add elements to the slide master, you can't move or resize the placeholders for the textboxes or pictures. If you try, they will appear to change but those changes won't take effect in the slides. Although you can have multiple slide masters with different design elements in them, you can't have multiple layouts of the data portion of the slides that exist in PowerPoint.

If you want the same design elements to appear on all your slide masters, such as having the same background theme, picture, or shape, then make those changes to the original slide master before adding additional masters. In this way those changes will copy over to the new masters you create. You can then do additional customization to those new slide masters.

See also

▸ The *Changing a slide's background color and theme* recipe

▸ The *Adding images to a slide* recipe

Adding audio to a slide

With all the concerns about literacy in the workplace, trainers need to create materials that can easily be used by workers with special requirements such as visual impairments or physical challenges. This also aids the visually impaired or those who have English as a second language. Quizmaker takes this into account, providing a way of narrating the questions and answer choices on every slide.

Getting ready

You will need a slide with a question on it to add your narrations to. You will need a microphone attached to your computer in order to record the narrations. A good quality microphone does make a difference as the sound quality will be better. Ideally, you want the microphone to be 3 to 6 inches in front of your mouth. This will vary if you are using a headset.

How to do it...

Audio narrations can add a lot to any presentation. They can also make the presentation or quiz more accessible to people who have disabilities or difficulties reading. To add audio to a slide, perform the following steps:

1. In the **Insert** section of the ribbon is a button for **Sound**. Clicking on this opens up a drop-down menu where you can choose to record or import sound. We're going to click on **Record Mic**.

2. This opens the **Record Microphone** dialog box, which is a simple recorder. This dialog box uses the standard symbols of a red spot for record, a blue triangle for play, and a blue square for stop, as shown in the following screenshot:

3. The first thing we want to do is to create a script, so click on the **Narration Script** button. Clicking on this button opens a small dialog box where you can type in your script. This can either be just the question and the answer choices or more complicated instructions, as required. When done, don't click on the **Close** button; leave it open so that you can use it.

4. Click on the red **Record** button in the **Record Microphone** dialog box. This will immediately start the recording. The band above it will act as a **Volume Unit** (**VU**) meter, showing you the relative recording volume.

5. Once you are done recording, click on the **Stop** button. This will have been grayed out but will change to blue when you start recording:

6. The legend in the band will change from **No audio** to **Ready** and the time at the right end of the band will change to show the actual number of seconds that your recording is of.

7. Play your narration back to check it. This is done by clicking on the **Play** button, which has a small blue triangle on it.

8. If your recording is not usable, you can delete it by clicking on the red **X** icon, which is now available.

9. To save your recording, click on the **Save** button on the recorder dialog box. Saving will close the dialog box.

10. In **Slide View**, an icon of a yellow speaker will appear outside of the slide image, in the lower-left corner of the window. Check to see if it is there.

How it works...

Although not visible, your recording will be saved as part of your slide. Now that you have a recording saved, the drop-down menu for sound will change, offering you the opportunity to play your narration, edit the sound, or remove it from the slide, as shown in the following screenshot:

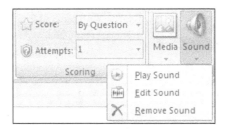

Adding video

Video is a great tool for any training or marketing application. We've already seen how video can be used in Articulate Presenter; now we're going to add a video to Quizmaker. The process is very similar to what we did in Presenter.

Getting ready

You'll need to have a quiz available to add the video to. If you have saved the quiz that we've been working on, you already have something available. If not, open Quizmaker and create at least one question. You need to be on the question window in order to add video.

How to do it...

Adding a video to a slide is very similar to adding a picture. However, there are some important differences, especially in selecting how the video will play. Perform the following steps:

1. Videos can be added in either **Form View** or **Slide View**. We're going to work in **Slide View** so that we can format the video, moving it to the exact location where we want it on the slide. If you are not currently in **Slide View**, click on **Slide View** in the ribbon.

2. Click on the **Insert** tab to locate the **Flash Movie** button; it will be in the **Media Clips** section of the ribbon. Clicking on this button opens a Windows open file dialog box so that you can locate the video you want to insert.

Remember that Articulate can only work with `.swf`, `.flv`, and `.mp4` video files. If your video is not in one of these formats, you can convert it with Articulate Video Encoder.

3. Once you've selected the video, click on the **OK** button to open the **Flash Movie Properties** dialog box, as shown in the following screenshot:

4. You can select for the movie to be displayed in the slide or in a new browser window. Let's select the **Display in a new browser window** radio button to have it displayed in a new browser window.

5. Let's also allow the viewer the ability to control the movie by clicking on the checkbox to the left-hand side of **Show movie controls**.

6. As we selected to allow the viewer to have access to movie controls, the dialog box changed, asking us about the browser window. Let's select **All browser controls** from the drop-down menu.

7. We can also adjust the movie volume. In most cases, the native volume of the movie will be too low unless it was professionally produced. So to increase it, let's click on the button to the right-hand side of **Sound volume** to open the slider. Then move the slider up to about three-quarters of the way up the scale.

8. When you are done, click on the **OK** button to add the video to the slide.

9. The video can be resized and moved on the slide. To resize it, grab one of the eight handles on the edges and drag it. Using a corner handle will keep the proportions of the video the same.

10. To move the video, click-and-hold anywhere on it, then drag-and-drop it to the correct location:

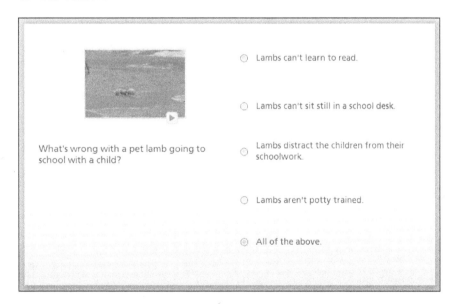

11. When you are finished adding your video, click on the **Save & Close** button on the ribbon to exit that slide. Note that the thumbnail of the slide has changed to show the video.

How it works...

While this is similar to adding video in Presenter, it isn't exactly the same. In Presenter, there is no capability for adding the movie player controls. In Quizmaker, there is no option to sync the video with the slide.

See also

> ▸   *Chapter 5, Taking Your Quiz to the Next Level*

5
Taking Your Quiz to the Next Level

In this chapter we will cover:

- ▸ Creating a simple storyline in Quizmaker
- ▸ Adding animation to your quiz
- ▸ Creating a branched story
- ▸ Creating a randomized question bank
- ▸ What about the results?
- ▸ Previewing and publishing your course or quiz

Introduction

In the last chapter we created a basic quiz to include different types of questions, images, audio, and even video. However, there's a lot more that we can do with Quizmaker.

Quizmaker will do much more than just create a quiz or survey; you can create an entire course in Quizmaker without using PowerPoint or Articulate Presenter. This would mean having to add slides with the information that is being presented as well as the quiz questions.

Branching allows you to create a storyline with multiple paths. Its most common use is for allowing different responses to a graded quiz question based upon which answer is selected. However, this branching capability gives you the ability to use quiz questions as a means to direct the user to various parts of the presentation where they will be presented with information specific to their needs.

One of its uses might be to provide product information in a trade show. Three different levels of information might be provided, as follows:

- Product features and benefits
- Product specifications
- Product costs and return-on-investment potential

This would allow the viewers to select the appropriate level of information for their particular needs, without having to go through all the other information. Customized presentations of this type have many other applications, both in sales and a corporate environment.

One of the things that makes Quizmaker unique from Presenter is its ability to score questions and tally those scores, providing a pass/fail grade. While Presenter does have some built-in capability to ask questions, the grading is on a per question basis with no build-in tallying and reporting capability. This scoring capability is the great difference between the two programs.

This grading capability also includes the ability to output those grades in a number of ways both to the user and via e-mail to others.

Finally, although Quizmaker is created as a standalone application, it is also designed to work in conjunction with Articulate Presenter. Quizzes created in Quizmaker can be published directly into a Presenter slide show, integrating the two programs together for even more options.

Creating a simple storyline in Quizmaker

Although Quizmaker is intended for use alongside Presenter, it is fully capable of working as a standalone package, creating complete Flash presentations. Doing so requires adding additional slides to the presentation, which aren't question slides.

When we use the term "storyline", we're not talking about using Quizmaker to tell a story, but in the sense of having a continuity of information presented along with the quiz and survey questions. This provides the capability of using Quizmaker to teach and immediately reinforce that teaching through a quiz. When used for surveys, information pertinent to the survey can be presented before questions are asked, helping to add clarity to the overall process. In the case of a sales presentation, questions can be asked for the purpose of directing the potential customer to the information that will best help them find what they are looking for.

The "storyline" concept provides a way of thinking for Quizmaker presentations with an eye towards creating flow and continuity. This helps to keep the interest of the users and helps the overall presentation make more sense to them.

Getting ready

You will need a presentation with a couple of questions already created. The type of questions that you use doesn't matter as we are going to add them to the existing quiz.

How to do it...

Creating a storyline consists of adding a series of slides to the quiz or survey, which provide information to the user. To create a storyline in Quizmaker perform the following steps:

1. From the Quizmaker main screen, click on the **New Blank Slide** button in the **Insert** section of the ribbon. This will add a slide to the presentation and open the **Slide Edit** screen:

2. The new slide will open in **Form View**. You can add information to the slide here, but it will be limited to the format of the master slide. Add a title for the slide and some text in the appropriate boxes.

3. You can add a picture or Flash movie by clicking on the **Media** button in the **Insert** section of the ribbon. Clicking on **Picture...** in the drop-down menu opens a Windows open file dialog box for you to select your picture from.

4. Switch to **Slide View** to see your slide and format it further. If you want more than one picture in the slide, the additional pictures have to be added in **Slide View**. This also allows formatting of the text, changing fonts, sizes, colors, and adding effects such as bold and underline:

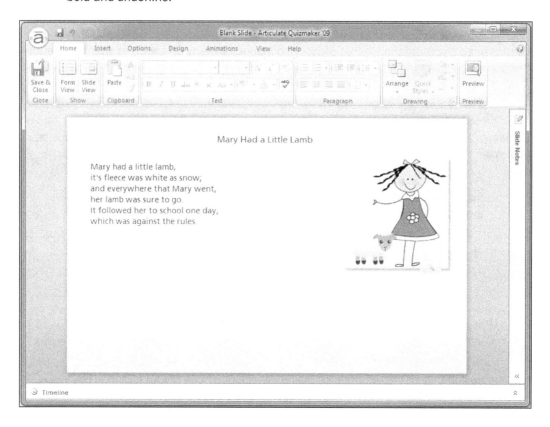

5. Formatting your slide in **Slide View** is much like working in PowerPoint. While not quite as robust, Quizmaker provides many of the same features located in the same ribbons that you can encounter in PowerPoint.

6. The default name on your slide will be **Blank Slide**. The slide name and title will appear to the right-hand side of the thumbnails in the main Quizmaker screen. To change the name return to **Form View**. There is a textbox for inserting the slide's name in the **Display** section of the ribbon. Enter the slide's name in the textbox.

7. Once your changes have been made, save the slide by clicking on the **Save & Close** button on the ribbon.

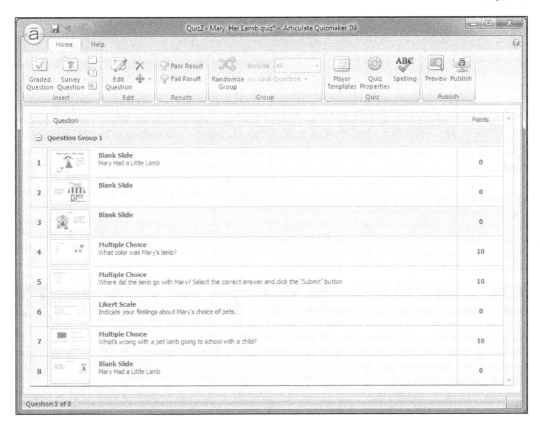

8. You can reorder your slides from the main Quizmaker screen by dragging-and-dropping them in the order that you want them to appear in.

How it works...

Adding blank slides allows the quiz creator to provide information to the viewer without having to include that information on the same slide as the questions. This can be useful in a number of ways, as follows:

- ▸ Teaching the individual who is taking the course, and then immediately testing him/her on that information for the purpose of reinforcing the lesson

- ▸ Providing examples on how to complete a problem and then allowing the learner a chance to practice that same sort of problem

- ▸ Providing background information for surveys before asking the questions
- ▸ In a sales presentation, presenting information about the product or products and then allowing the viewer the opportunity to select whether they want further information, specifications, a product demonstration video, or the opportunity to see other products

It is important to remember that as far as Quizmaker is concerned, each slide is a question. While this will not affect an individual's score, it can cause some problems when providing questions from a question bank (we'll talk about that in the *Creating a randomized question bank* recipe).

See also

- ▸ The *Creating a randomized question bank* recipe
- ▸ The *Creating a branched story* recipe

Adding animation to your quiz

Adding animation to the objects in a slide can do a lot to make that slide more interesting. While that may not seem as important as the content, it does help keep the learner's attention and focus on the lesson or quiz.

Getting ready

You'll need a quiz question. It can be either a graded quiz or a survey quiz. You'll also need a couple of objects in it. If you still have the quiz where you added an image in the *Adding images to a slide* recipe in *Chapter 4, Creating Assessments and Courses with Quizmaker*, you can use that. All we'll need to do is add another object.

How to do it...

To animate images and objects perform the following steps:

1. **Form View** limits us to only adding one picture, so let's switch over to **Slide View** as shown in the following screenshot:

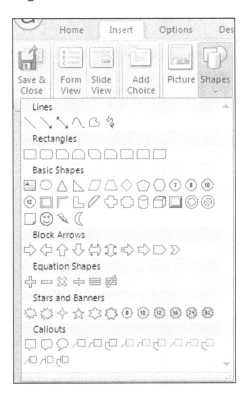

 Since we're making these changes in **Slide View**, it's important to ensure that we're not covering up any part of the question or answer choices. If we do, we can either move it or arrange the object to the back. To move it to the back, click on the object, click on the **Format** tab, and click on the **Send to Back** icon in the **Arrange** section.

2. In the **Animations** tab on the ribbon, there are two types of animations, namely **Entrance Animations** and **Exit Animations**. Click on the rectangle, and then click on the star-shaped button in the **Entrance Animations** area of the ribbon. This will open a dropbox where you can select the **Fade In** animation, as shown in the following screenshot:

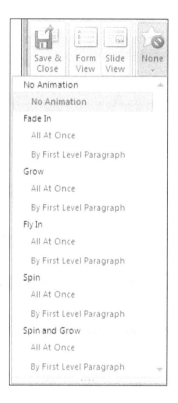

3. Select an animation. The star-shaped button will now change from yellow to green and the name of the animation will be below it.

4. Change the speed of the animation to **Fast** by using the **Speed** drop-down menu.

5. To add an exit animation, repeat the last three steps using the star-shaped button in the **Exit Animations** section of the ribbon.

6. Click on the image and select **Fly In** as the animation. For this animation, it is necessary to select the direction that it comes in from. Click on the **Enter From** drop-down menu and select the left-pointing arrow, which will bring the image in from the right border of the slide.

 It is a good idea to prevent your image animations from covering the text when entering and exiting.

7. Now let's set the timing for the animation. Click on **Timeline** located on the bottom bar of the window to open the **Timeline** section of the window. You will see everything listed in the slide along with a timeline in seconds across the top of the pane.

> It is not necessary to use both entrance and exit animations. You can choose to bring an animation in and leave it there. If you want the viewer to only be able to look at the image for a predetermined time, you can use an exit animation to make it leave after this time.

8. Click on the **Timeline** section of **Shape 1**. This will cause it to be highlighted in yellow. Click-and-hold on the right end of the timeline, and then drag it to the 5-second line to shorten the amount of time that the shape is on the slide. Both the entrance and exit transitions will be completed in that time period.

9. Click on the **Timeline** section of **Picture 1**. This time grab the left edge of the timeline and drag it to the right-hand side, to the 5-second mark. This will make it so that the picture doesn't appear until after the shape has entered and exited.

10. Check your animation sequencing by clicking on the **Play** button in the lower-left corner of the window, as shown in the following screenshot:

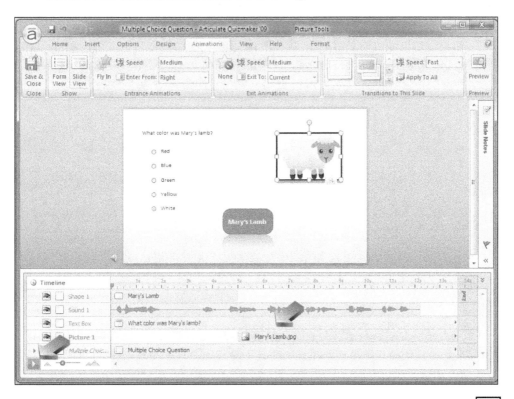

11. Click on the **Save & Close** button on the ribbon to return to the list of slides and select your next slide to animate or add another question to the quiz.

How it works...

The timeline allows you to make your animations more interesting and sync them to the information in the narration. In this way, you can make the slide instructional instead of just a quiz question. Another way that you can use this is to have images for each of the answer choices, illustrating the choice.

There's more...

Animations aren't just limited to the actions that happen within the slide, but the slide transitions as well. This is a powerful tool for making the presentation more attractive and interesting to the viewer.

A word of caution on animating transitions. If too many different animations are used, it detracts from the professionalism of the presentation, confusing the viewer.

Adding slide transitions

Unlike Presenter, which doesn't allow slide transitions, Quizmaker does have a number of built-in transitions. To add slide transitions perform the following steps:

1. These transitions are also located on the **Animations** ribbon. Clicking on the button at the bottom of the **Transitions** scroll bar opens the fly-out menu, allowing you to select the transition that you want, as shown in the following screenshot:

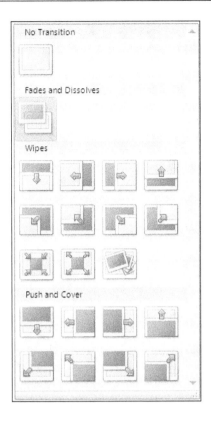

2. The transition speed can be changed by selecting the **Speed** drop-down menu and selecting the setting you want.

3. When using transitions, some uniformity helps with the branding of the presentation. By clicking on the **Apply to All** button in the **Transitions to This Slide** section of the ribbon, you can use the same transition throughout the presentation.

Creating a branched story

Branching provides a way of directing the viewer to a particular slide, which may not be the next slide in the presentation. It is referred to as branching because the slide can be changed depending upon the answer that the user selects for a particular question. In its simplest form, branching would take a user who gives the right answer to one location and to another location for a wrong answer.

This idea can be expanded upon by using multiple-choice questions as a directory, to direct the user to one of several different locations. It can also be used in a quiz situation to provide an opportunity for the learner to review the information and retake the question if they get it wrong.

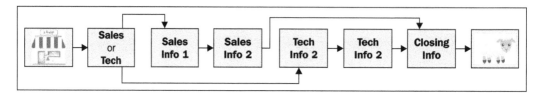

Branching always takes the user to another slide within the presentation. This is selectable for each answer. By allowing branching at every question, extremely complicated presentations can be made, customizing the presentation according to the needs of the viewer.

Getting ready

You will need a quiz with at least one question and at least two blank slides with something on them. If you saved your work from the last recipe, it will work perfectly for this, or you can open a quiz that you have created and add some blank slides with information on them.

How to do it...

Branching works from the feedback and the **Branching** section at the bottom of **Form View** in the **Question Feedback** screen. It can be done from either a question or blank slide. To create a branched story perform the following steps:

1. Open a quiz question from the main screen of Quizmaker by double-clicking on it.
2. At the bottom of **Form View**, you'll see the **SET FEEDBACK AND BRANCHING** section. For a quiz question, there will be two options—**Correct** and **Incorrect**. For blank slides and survey questions, there will only be one option.

 Branching can only be done from **Form View** and not from **Slide View**.

3. Click on the **More...** button to the right-hand side of the **Incorrect** option. This will open the **Question Feedback** dialog box, as shown in the following screenshot:

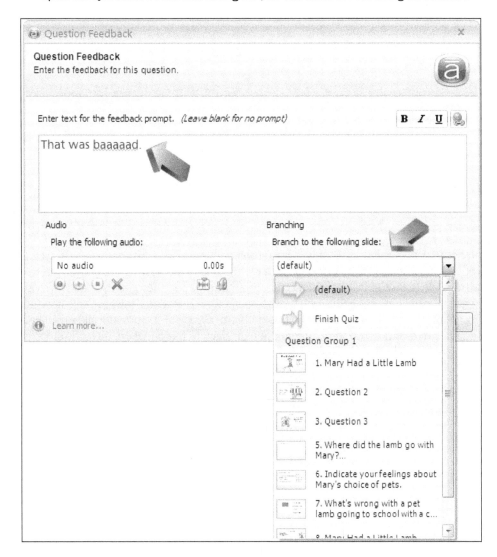

4. Remove the text for the feedback by highlighting and hitting the *Delete* key on your keyboard.

5. Click on the **Branch to the following slide** drop-down menu in the **Branching** section of the dialog box. This will show you the various options from where you can have the program take the user for an incorrect answer. The **(default)** setting will take them to the next slide in the presentation. We're going to have them directed to a review slide, as shown in the flow chart in the *How it works...* section of this recipe.

6. Click on the **OK** button. This will apply the change.

7. Once you have created the branch, an icon will appear to the left-hand side of the **More...** button to show that the quiz has been branched, as shown in the following screenshot:

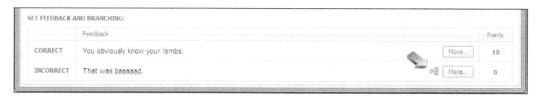

8. Click on the **Save & Close** button in the **Question Feedback** screen to save the changes to the presentation.

How it works...

Remember that the branching that you create will happen every time that a viewer cycles through the presentation. It is very easy to make the mistake of having the viewer return to review the slide that originally presented the information when they get an answer wrong, and then place a branch at that point, which goes back to the question. However, this can mess up the original presentation order. To avoid this problem, a copy of the original slide may have to be used for the review, which then directs the user back to the question, as follows:

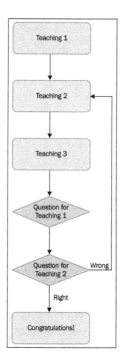

As you can see from this flowchart, a wrong answer for the question on teaching 2 takes the learner back to teaching 2. However, the learner would then have to review teaching 3 and retake question 1 as well. To avoid this, a copy of teaching 2 should be made, which can be used for the review, and the learner should then be redirected back to question 2, as follows:

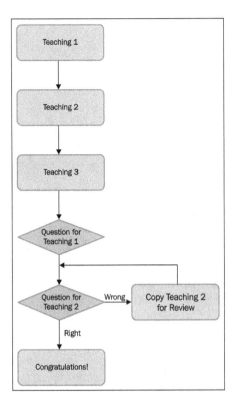

As you can see, by making this change the learner is provided with the opportunity to review the information and retake the question without affecting the rest of the presentation. While this makes the overall course a little larger, it works better.

Creating a randomized question bank

When testing a group of students, it can be helpful to vary the questions between tests. This is a common way of fighting against cheating, whether by looking at the test of the person next to you or by working off a list of answers that someone else has prepared. Unfortunately, creating several versions of the same test creates a lot of extra work for the trainer, work that they really don't have time to do.

Quizmaker solves this problem by providing access to randomized questions. This is done out of a question bank, where x number of questions are selected out of the y number in the bank. In this way, each test is individualized while still keeping all the tests fair.

Getting ready

We're going to start with a blank graded quiz. So open Quizmaker and select **Create a new quiz** on the startup screen. In the **New Quiz** dialog box, select **Graded Quiz** and click on the **OK** button.

When the main screen opens, take a look at the main part of the screen. You'll notice that there is a heading called **Question Group 1**. Quizmaker uses question groups to know which questions you need to select from.

How to do it...

In order to provide something for Quizmaker to choose from, we're going to have to create several questions. To create a randomized question bank, perform the following steps:

1. Click on **Graded Question** on the ribbon and create a question. Actually, you need to create a number of questions so that the program can choose between them.

2. Notice that all these questions are located under the heading **Question Group 1**. This is important as we want the program to select from this group.

3. Double-click on the legend **Question Group 1**. This will open a textbox, containing the legend **Question Group 1**. Change the name by erasing what is there and typing in a new name.

4. Click on the **Randomize Group** button in the **Group** section of the ribbon. The words **Randomize all questions** will appear next to the group name.

5. In the **Include** drop-down menu next to the **Randomize Group** button, select the number of questions that you want the program to ask the learner. The legend next to the group name will change to read "Randomize, include x questions".

6. Add another group by clicking on the **New Question Group** button in the **Insert** section of the ribbon.

7. Add a blank slide to question group 2. To make sure that the blank slide is added to the correct group, the group must be highlighted. Simply click on it to highlight it. The bar that is highlighted will be darker than the other group bars:

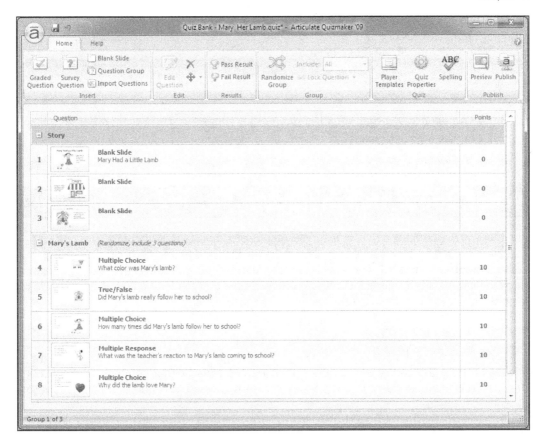

8. Move the new group (group 2) above the first group by dragging-and-dropping the bar that says "question group 2". All the slides in the group will move with it.

How it works...

Quizmaker selects from all the questions that are contained within a question group. It does not recognize blank slides and treats them as if they were questions. Therefore, it is important to separate the blank slides from the question slides by putting them in separate groups.

You can have several groups in a quiz. This allows you to select the program from several question banks. You might want to have a group of 10 multiple-choice questions, of which five are used. Following that, you might want to add another group of 10 multiple-choice questions, of which eight are chosen. Then you might want to add a third group of questions in which all of them are used. By grouping the questions, you are able to control exactly how Quizmaker presents them to the learner.

You can also create a question group for the slides that are used specifically for branching. That will keep them out of any question bank and group them together for easy recognition when reviewing or modifying the presentation.

See also

▸ The *Adding a basic graded question* recipe in *Chapter 4, Creating Assessments and Courses with Quizmaker*

▸ The *Creating a simple storyline in Quizmaker* recipe

What about the results?

Whether you are creating a quiz or a survey, results are important. Without them you're just wasting your time and the user's time. Quizmaker is designed to interface with a **learning management system** (**LMS**) and will provide the results to that. However, this doesn't mean that the learners aren't interested in their own results or that the learners may not need to send them to their instructor. Quizmaker provides these options.

Getting ready

The results for a quiz can be set up at any point in the process, either before or after creating the questions or blank slides. You can either work from a new, blank quiz or from one that you have already created.

How to do it...

Quiz results are for the entire quiz, so you set them up from the main Quizmaker screen and not from any particular question or blank slide. There are two different buttons, one for **Pass Result** and one for **Fail Result** on the ribbon. To set up the quiz results perform the following steps:

1. Click on the **Pass Result** button on the ribbon. This will open the **Results Slide** screen. The screen will open in **Form View**, as shown in the following screenshot:

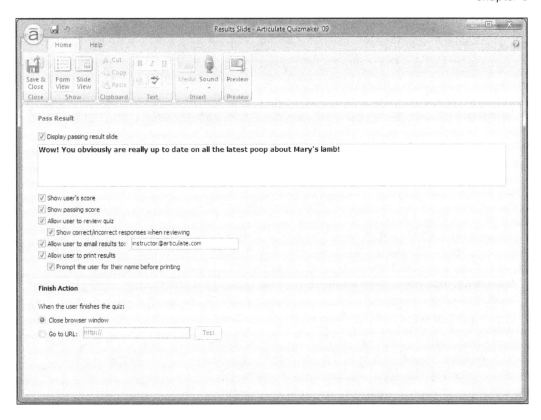

2. There are a number of checkboxes to select, which determine what will be shown on the **Results Slide** window. The first thing you need to decide is whether or not you want the results slide to show. This is the first checkbox. If you decide not to show the results, all the other selections are grayed out.

3. Let's select everything so that the results slide will have everything on it.

4. To have the results e-mailed to the instructor, the instructor's e-mail address must be inserted in the textbox next to **Allow user to email results to**.

5. You can add sound to the slide either in the form of narration or sound effects. To add a sound effect, click on the **Sound** button on the ribbon and then select **Import Sound...**. This will open a Windows open file dialog box with which you can find the sound file.

6. Once the sound has been imported, it can be edited. The **Sound** icon will change from a microphone to a speaker. Clicking on it will open a drop-down menu where you can select the sound editor:

7. At the bottom of the screen, there is the **Finish Action** section for selecting the final action to be taken by the program once the user has had a chance to review the results. To direct the user to a page on a website, select the radio button for **Go to URL**, and type in or paste the URL for the page in the textbox.

8. It is always a good idea to ensure that the URL is entered correctly, by clicking on the **Test** button.

9. Once all the information is selected, click on **Slide View** to see how the slide will appear. You can reformat the information on the slide in any way that you want, including adding pictures and backgrounds.

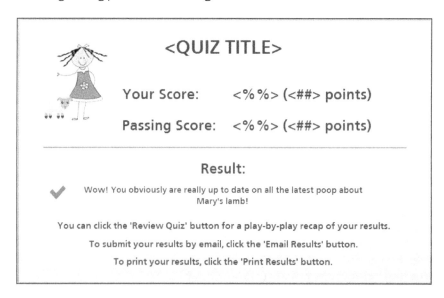

Whatever you do, don't change any of the information that is included within the brackets **< >**. This is necessary for coding so that Quizmaker can input the results into the slide.

10. When you are done changing the slide, click on the **Save & Close** button on the ribbon to save it.

11. Perform the same steps for **Fail Result**. You may choose to provide different options, such as not e-mailing the results to the instructor.

How it works...

The results of the quiz are tallied automatically through the course of the quiz. This screen allows the user to see the results of their quiz immediately. This same information can be printed out or provided to the instructor via e-mail.

Quizmaker doesn't act as an e-mail server; it only provides a link to the individual's default e-mail account. So when the learner clicks on the button to e-mail the results, it will take them to their default e-mail.

Since different results can be selected for passing and failing the course, a learner who doesn't pass can be directed to review the information via the information's URL and then back to the quiz for a second try.

There's more...

Since Quizmaker can be used to create both quizzes and surveys, the results for surveys are graded and presented differently than for quizzes, although the process for setting up the response is similar.

Setting up results for surveys

This option would only apply if you have created a survey quiz rather than a graded quiz. That is done at the beginning, when you select **New Quiz**. To set up the results for surveys, perform the following steps:

1. Instead of seeing buttons for **Pass Result** and **Fail Result** on the ribbon, you will have a single button that says **Survey Result**. Click on this; the **Results Slide** screen will open as shown in the following screenshot:

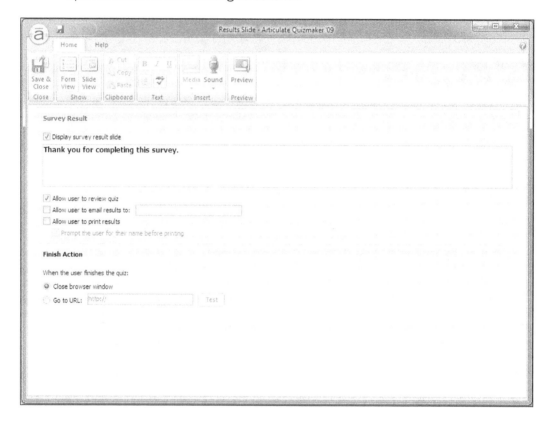

2. There are fewer selections that can be made on this screen than there are for the pass and fail results. However, the selections are made in the same way.

See also

▶ The *Adding audio to a slide* recipe in *Chapter 4, Creating Assessments and Courses with Quizmaker*

- The *Adding images to a slide* recipe in *Chapter 4, Creating Assessments and Courses with Quizmaker*

- The *Changing a slide's background color and theme* recipe from *Chapter 4, Creating Assessments and Courses with Quizmaker*

Previewing and publishing your course or quiz

Just like Articulate Presenter, Quizmaker creates a Flash video presentation of your quiz or survey. This requires that the program publish the quiz, outputting the information that you created as the Flash video.

Getting ready

You will need a quiz that you have already created. It doesn't matter whether it is a graded quiz or survey quiz, nor does it matter how long it is.

How to do it...

Although you can preview any individual slide as you are working on it, you must publish the quiz from the main Quizmaker screen. To preview and publish your course or quiz perform the following steps:

1. Click on the **Preview** button in the **Publish** section of the ribbon. It will take a few minutes for Quizmaker to produce your preview, because it is doing everything that it needs to do for publishing, except making the files.

2. The preview that is created is a working preview, allowing you to test out the functions, including the answers to the questions. Cycle through your quiz by clicking on the **NEXT** button on the lower-right corner of the skin.

3. Unless you have deselected the feedback on any slide, you will receive feedback on each question. At the end of the quiz, you will receive your score, as shown in the following screenshot:

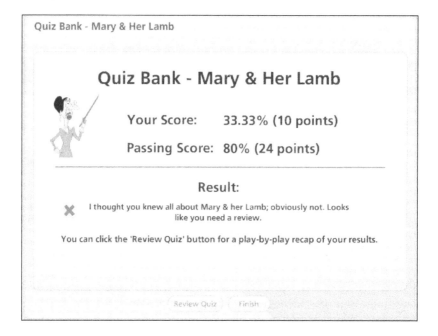

4. You can review the quiz again if you want to, by clicking on the **Review Quiz** button on the ribbon. You can also select to view a particular slide by clicking on the **Select** button on the ribbon.

5. If you find an error, clicking on the **Edit Question** button will return you to the editor.

6. When done reviewing the slides, click on the **Close Preview** button to return to the main screen.

7. Click on the **Publish** button on the ribbon. This will open the same **Publish** dialog box that we had in Presenter, with one difference. There is an **ARTICULATE PRESENTER** tab for publishing to Articulate Presenter, as shown in the following screenshot:

8. If you have multiple PowerPoint presentations open, they will show in the first textbox where you will need to select the correct presentation.

9. The only thing you have to decide here is whether to have the quiz published as a slide in the presentation or a tab in the player. If you select **Insert as a tab in the player**, it will appear in the upper-right corner of the player.

10. Click on **Publish**. It will take several minutes for Quizmaker to publish your quiz as a Flash video presentation.

How it works...

The program has to follow almost the same process for creating a preview as it does for publishing the presentation. The difference is that in publishing, the files are saved to the computer's hard drive, while when a preview is created, the files are only tiles in the computer's short term (RAM) memory.

See also

▶ The *Previewing and publishing your course* recipe in *Chapter 3, Preparing Your Player*

6
Creating Interactive Content with Engage

In this chapter we will cover:

- ▶ Setting up an Engage template
- ▶ Step-by-step approach for a Process interaction
- ▶ Adding images and video in Engage
- ▶ Adding and editing audio
- ▶ Using Engage to create a glossary
- ▶ Creating a labeled graphic
- ▶ Previewing and publishing your interaction

Introduction

The Internet today is becoming more and more interactive. Nowhere is this more obvious than on educational websites. Simply providing information for the learner to read has given way to providing a learning experience where they can interact with the website. This helps keep the learners engaged and increases their comprehension of the material being presented.

The third part of the Articulate suite is called Engage. This program provides the capability of creating interactive activities for the viewer. These can be used either as standalone items on websites, or they can be published to Articulate Presenter and included as part of an entire presentation.

In this chapter, we're going to learn how to use this powerful but simple tool to create interactive content for our presentations and websites.

While Articulate Engage can be used as a standalone package for creating interactive activities, glossaries, and graphics, it is predominantly designed to create these items for use with Presenter. Each interactive activity is handled separately and without Presenter to string them together, and they don't have any connection with one another.

In Presenter, the interactions can be displayed as a slide or as a tab. While presenting them as a slide is better for most interactions, it makes more sense to provide an interactive glossary as a tab on the skin so that the viewer can access it at any time.

To access Articulate Engage, click on the icon on your desktop. If you do not have the icon on your desktop, you can also access it from the **Articulate** ribbon in PowerPoint, as shown in the following screenshot:

Engage's opening screen will provide options such as **Create a new interaction** and **Open a recent interaction**.

Setting up an Engage template

Like the other Articulate packages, Engage works off a template. This provides the style for the presentation, allowing for company or series branding. While the template is not as complex as it is for Presenter or QuizMaker, there are still a number of things that can be done to the template.

There are a number of built-in templates, which provide a starting point for establishing the style of the presentation. These can either be used as they are, or they can be modified to meet your needs. Whenever you modify a template, Engage will ask you for a new name to save it under.

Getting ready

You will need Engage open, ready to create a new interaction. For the sake of simplicity, we're going to use a Process interaction. However, the steps we are performing are independent of the type of interaction, so the same thing could be done from any of the interaction types.

How to do it...

We will be working with two tools, **Colors** and **Interaction Properties**, both of which are located in the **Tools** portion of the ribbon, as shown in the following screenshot:

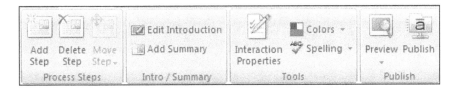

To set up an Engage template perform the following steps:

1. Click on the **Colors** button on the ribbon; this will open the **Colors** drop-down menu. You will notice that it is divided into two sections—**Schemes** and **Legacy Schemes**. They are all color schemes that can be used in Engage. The legacy schemes are fancier than the standard schemes.

2. Select the first legacy scheme, which is called **Blue Cool**, by clicking on it:

3. Now let's modify this color scheme. To do so, click on the legend **New Color Scheme** located at the bottom of the **Colors** drop-down menu. This will open the **Color Scheme Editor** window.

4. At the bottom of the **Color Scheme Editor** window, there are three controls such as **Choose an item to edit**, **Color**, and **Transparency**. Click on the box that says **Background** to open a list of items that you can select custom colors for, as shown in the following screenshot:

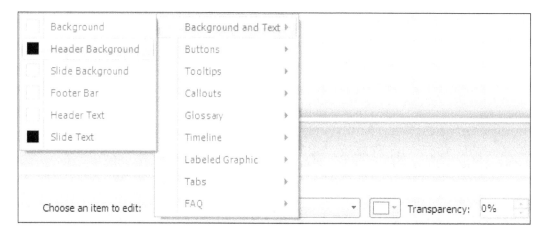

5. In this case, we're going to select **Header Background** from the **Background and Text** category.

 You may notice that the **Transparency** setting disappears when you select some items for editing. That's done to keep Engage compatible with Presenter. A semitransparent background may render some items unreadable when placed over a background graphic in Presenter. So for those items, the transparency cannot be set.

6. Clicking on the color block to the right of where you selected the item to be edited opens up a color selection fly-out menu, where you can select the color that you want that item to be, as shown in the following screenshot:

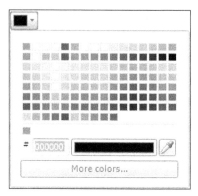

7. Repeat this selection process for each of the other items in the color scheme.

8. When you are finished making changes to the color scheme, click on the **OK** button. This will open a small dialog box asking you to name your color scheme. Once you've named the scheme, click on the **OK** button to save it.

9. The other area we need to customize for the scheme is **Interaction Properties**. Click on the **Interaction Properties** button on the ribbon to open the dialog box.

10. In the **Playback** tab, let's select the radio button next to **Interactive – user can advance in any order** to allow the viewers the most freedom in selecting how they view the presentation. Since we are trying to give them the most freedom to interact with the presentation, let's also click on the checkbox next to **Show previous/next buttons**. Note that this tab will be the same for all the interaction types:

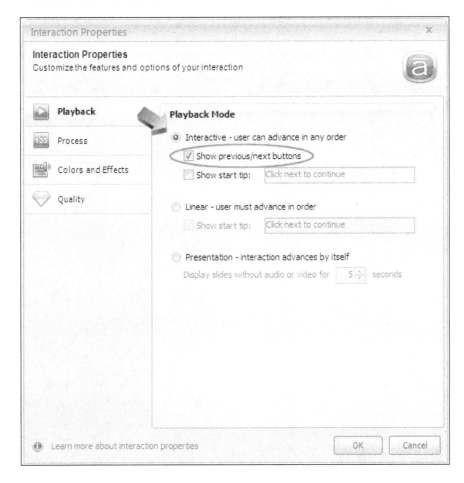

11. Click on the **Process** tab. This tab will change for each interaction type. Here we can select the features that we want visible. Let's check the **Introduction** and **Summary** checkboxes by selecting them and deselecting the others.

12. In the lower part of this tab, click on the drop-down menu to select the numbering style that you want used for your presentation.

13. Click on the **Colors and Effects** tab. If we had not already selected the color scheme, we could do so here. Select **Animation Style** of **Fade** and change **Media Borders** to **Drop Shadow**. To eliminate the clicking sound effects when the users click on their mouse buttons in the presentation, click on the **Play sound effects** checkbox, to deselect it, as shown in the following screenshot:

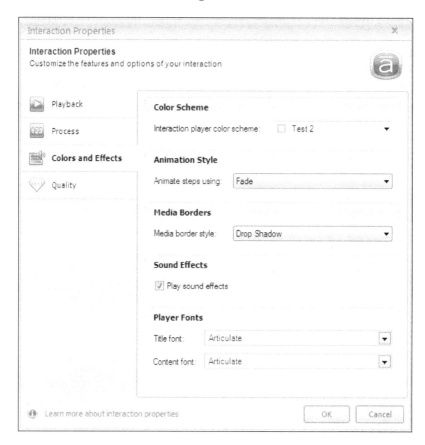

14. Click on the **Quality** tab. This contains the same choices that are in Presenter. For more information on this, refer to the *Setting up course defaults* recipe in *Chapter 3, Preparing Your Player*.

How it works...

Like the other parts of the Articulate suite, Engage also produces a Flash video file.

The color schemes you create in the editor aren't just for the presentation you are working on at the moment. They become part of the color scheme library. Once you've created a new color scheme, it will show up in the drop-down menu whenever you click on the **Colors** button in the **Tools** section of the ribbon. As you can see here, I've created two new color schemes called **Test** and **Test 2**; they show up under the **Custom Schemes** heading, as shown in the following screenshot:

There's more...

In addition to selecting colors by clicking on the color in the fly-out menu, you can type in the HTML color number. The color in the bar to the right-hand side of the number will change to show you the color you have selected.

 There are some excellent resources online, such as ColorPicker.com, that help in determining the HTML color code for colors. One selects their color and the code appears in a window above the color selector. This code can then be copied into the Engage color fly-out menu.

You can also use an eyedropper to select any color off your computer screen. Simply click on the button for eyedropper (circled in red in the following screenshot), and then click on the color you want selected. This is not limited to colors in Engage but includes any color that is on your computer's screen:

Once the eyedropper button is selected from the color chooser, move the mouse pointer to any color on your screen and click there. Please note that the mouse pointer will not change to look like an eyedropper.

See also

▶ The *Setting up course defaults* recipe in *Chapter 3, Preparing Your Player*

Step-by-step approach for a Process interaction

Basically all of the types of interactions work in the same way, with the exception of the Labeled Graphic and Glossary interactions. The differences in the rest are minor enough so that they are easily recognizable and intuitive. So we're going to do a Process interaction as an example. From that you should be fine to do the other types. The majority of the difference between the various types is in how the program graphically presents the information.

A Process interaction takes the viewer through a series of steps, providing information about each step. As such it is excellent for explaining instructions on how to complete a task. Each step can be shown thoroughly, in order, allowing the viewer to see the entire process.

Getting ready

You'll need to have Articulate Engage open to do this. On the opening screen, click on **Create a new interaction**. This will open the **New Interaction** dialog box.

How to do it...

Articulate Engage simplifies the process of creating these interactive slides for you. As the creator, you are providing the information, which fits into the standard interactive templates that Engage has. To do a Process interaction perform the following steps:

1. From the **New Interaction** dialog box, select the **Process** tab, which is the first tab in the list. Click on the **OK** button to go into the editor.
2. The first thing you need to edit is the name of the interaction. The textbox for **Interaction Title** will say **Process** (or whatever type of interaction you've selected). Type in the name of your interaction.
3. In the editor, you'll see a number of tabs for the various steps located above the text-editing section. These tabs are for selecting the actual steps that you will be editing the information for. Select the tab for the first step. In the following screenshot, it says **1. Mary & Her Lamb**. Notice that it is darkened to show that it is selected:

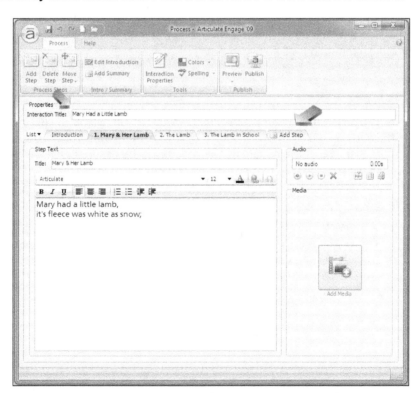

4. Change the name of the tab by typing a title for it in the textbox labeled **Title**.

5. Add text to the step by clicking in the text editor and typing in the text. The editor provides the full ability to edit the font, size, color, bullet and numbered lists, and make it bold and aligned.

6. Repeat this process for each of the steps in your Process interaction.

7. If you need to add additional steps (which will show up as additional tabs) to the process, you can click on the **Add Step** tab or the **Add Step** button on the ribbon. You can also remove tabs by clicking on the **Delete Step** button on the ribbon.

8. You can move tabs, reordering them in the process by dragging-and-dropping them into a new location in the list of tabs. The tab will automatically get renumbered in its new location.

9. To add an introduction or summary, click on the appropriate buttons on the ribbon. These are edited in the same manner as the steps.

10. Once you have finished adding all your text, click on the **Spelling** button on the ribbon to check the spelling of the entire process. It does not matter which tab you are in when you use a spellcheck, as it will check the entire process.

How it works...

The information you are providing will be used by Engage to create the Process interaction. The same thing can be done for each of the other types of interactions. The major difference relates to how the information will be displayed.

There's more...

At times it might be necessary to add symbols to the text. The Omega button (Ω) in the text editor allows the addition of common symbols. If the symbol you need does not appear in the list, click on **More Symbols** at the bottom of the list to open the character map, where you can select any symbol contained in any font on your computer.

Graphic interactions

For some types of interactions, the information is presented in a graphic, with the text in a box associated with each segment of that graphic. Clicking on that segment of the graphic causes the information associated with that segment to appear, as shown in the following screenshot:

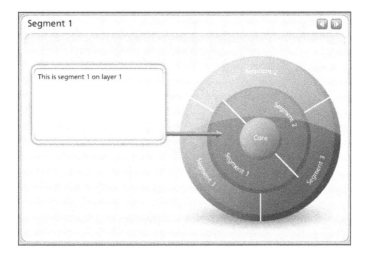

You can add layers and segments to the graphic with the **Add Layer** and **Add Segment** buttons on the ribbon.

The Timeline interaction works in the same way, with the exception of the form that the information is presented in.

Adding images and video in Engage

As with any other presentation, it's easier to keep the viewer's interest if you have some graphics. Engage makes it possible to add one graphic or video to each step in the process or each item of text in the Graphics-based interactions.

These graphics can be used simply to add interest or illustrate a point. In a Timeline interaction, each point on the time line could have an image that illustrates the event at that point in time.

Getting ready

You'll need Engage open, with an interaction that you've already started working on. If you have the Process interaction, which we used for the last recipe, then you can use it, adding images to the existing steps.

How to do it...

Each step can display one image or video clip. There is no way to show multiple images in one step or one part of a Graphic interaction.

In the **Media** section of the editing screen, click on the **Add Media** button, or the legend **Add Media** that is below it.

 Images must be in the `.jpg`, `.gif`, `.png`, or `.bmp` formats to work with Engage.

To add images and video in Engage, perform the following steps:

1. This will open a standard, Windows open file dialog box. Select the image that you want and then click on the **Open** button. This will open the **Multimedia Properties** dialog box. A thumbnail of the image you selected will appear in the dialog box, as shown in the following screenshot:

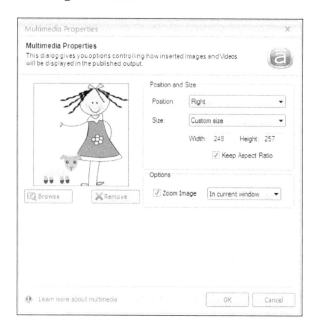

2. The default location for the graphic will appear as **Right**, and the default size will be set to **Auto-size**. You can change the size by clicking on the **Size** drop-down menu and selecting **Custom size**. This will open additional textboxes where you can input the width and height.

3. Input the new width and height that you want the image to be displayed with in pixels. As long as **Keep Aspect Ratio** is checked, changing the size of one will automatically cause the other to change in proportion to it.

 The size of the image is somewhat limited. If you select a size that is too large, when you click on **OK**, you will see a message telling you that the size you have chosen is too large and what the maximum size you can use is.

4. In the **Options** section of the dialog box, check **Zoom Image** for the viewer to be able to zoom the image. Then select **In current window** to have it zoom in the current window.

5. Click on the **OK** button to add this image to your interaction. The button on the main screen will be replaced by a thumbnail of the image you have just selected. The legend **Edit Properties** will display below the thumbnail, allowing you to make changes to the location and size.

How it works...

Engage will add the image to the process steps or graphic when it produces the Flash video. If you would like to see how it will appear, you can do so at any time by creating a preview. The preview will do everything the final Flash video file does, but it will not be saved.

There's more...

Articulate Engage allows you to add both images and video. These are both categorized together under the name "Media".

Adding video

Adding video to Engage is essentially the same as adding images. The only difference is that when adding video, you need to select the necessary settings for video. Perform the following steps to add video:

1. Add the video in the same way that an image is added.

2. When the **Multimedia Properties** dialog box opens, it will have a section for **Options**. Check the checkbox next to **Include Playbar**, if you would like to allow the viewer to be able to go back and review sections of the video.

3. If you select **Include Playbar**, you will also be allowed to select **Auto Start**. If not, the **Auto Start** selection will be grayed out.

Remember that Articulate only works with Flash video formats and the `.mp4` format. So your videos must be in the `.swf`, `.flv`, or `.mp4` formats. If they are not already in those formats, they can be converted using Articulate Video Encoder.

See also

▸ *Chapter 7, Basic Video Editing with Video Encoder*

Adding and editing audio

Like the other Articulate products, audio narration can be added in Engage. However, there is no provision for a music track. If you want to have music, you would need to edit the soundtrack outside of Engage and then import it as audio.

Getting ready

You'll need an interaction that you can work with. If you still have the one that you've been using for the other recipes in this chapter, you can use it. If not, create a new interaction of any type. I'll be explaining it with a process interaction, but the procedure is the same regardless of the interaction type.

You'll need to have a microphone attached to your computer to record with. A good-quality microphone makes a difference, as it will generally produce a clearer sound with less noise. You also need a quiet environment; if you can hear something, there's a good chance that it will be picked up by the microphone as well. Barking dogs, noisy air conditioners, and kids playing can all ruin a recording.

How to do it...

Each step or each part of a graphic's audio narration will have to be recorded individually. The same process is used for each step, regardless of how many steps you have. You can also do the same thing for the **Introduction** and **Summary** sections. To add and edit audio perform the following steps:

1. Locate the **Audio** section on the main Engage screen. It is circled in the following screenshot:

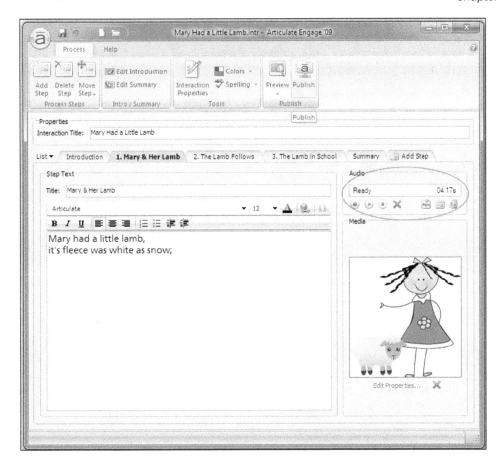

2. Before recording, it's always a good idea to know what you are going to say. Click on the **Narration Script** button below the text area in the **Audio** section of the screen. This is the second button from the right-hand side.

3. Enter your narration script into the textbox. Like any other textbox in Windows, it can be repositioned to a convenient location on your screen, where you can see it easily while recording.

4. To record, click on the round, red **Record** button below the textbox in the **Audio** section of the screen. The program will start recording your audio immediately. To stop, click on the **Stop** button, which has a blue square on it. The recording will automatically be saved.

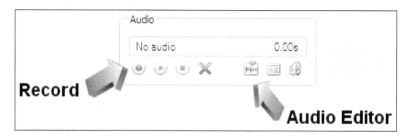

5. Check your recording by clicking on the **Play** Button, which has a blue triangle on it.

6. To edit your recording, click on the **Audio Editor** button, which is the third button from the right-hand side; this will open the **Audio Editor** window.

7. You can trim off any excessive silence at the beginning and end of the narration by highlighting the section to be removed and clicking on the **Delete** button on the ribbon.

8. If you need to add silence, you can do so by positioning the cursor where you want the silence to be added and then click on the **Silence** button on the ribbon. Input the number of seconds of silence you want to add, and then click on the **OK** button as shown in the following screenshot:

9. You will probably need to adjust the volume level of your narration. The waveform should almost touch the top and bottom of the white area in the editor, without getting all the way to the top and bottom. If it does not, click on the **Volume** button on the ribbon to adjust the volume. This will open a dialog box with a slider for adjusting the volume.

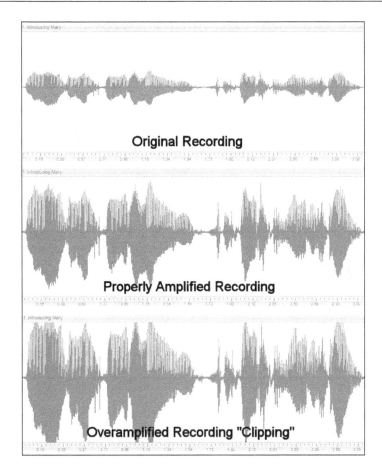

Original Recording

Properly Amplified Recording

Overamplified Recording "Clipping"

10. You can only increase the volume by up to 100 percent. However if that still isn't enough, you can amplify it again by repeating step 9 as many times as necessary.

How it works...

Audio is not only a great way to make your presentation user friendly, but it's essential when trying to make it disability friendly. However, good-quality audio recordings are important. Otherwise you're better off not having them. If the viewer can't hear what is being said in the narration, either because it's not loud enough or because of the background noise, they won't use the narration and may ignore the presentation altogether.

Good-quality narration requires only a few ingredients, as follows:

- A quiet area for recording; background noise can be very distracting.
- A decent-quality microphone; avoid using the mike in your webcam, as the distance it is at from your mouth will tend to make you sound like you're in a tunnel. The ideal distance for a microphone is 6 inches from your mouth.
- Speaking clearly and slowly; however you don't want to be too slow, as it will make the presentation boring and tedious.
- Editing your narration to remove unnecessary noise and quiet moments.
- High volume without distortion; always check this.

Everyone's voice changes throughout the day. What you eat, drink, how tired you are, and how much you've spoken will affect how it sounds. Ideally, you want to record everything in one session to keep it consistent. If you can't record it all at the same time, record it during the same time of day and try to repeat everything so that your physical condition and environment are the same.

There's more...

If you have professionally recorded narrations, they can be imported into Articulate Engage. To do so, click on the **Import Audio File** button, which looks like a yellow speaker button in the **Audio** section, and select the file.

 You can only import the `.wav` and `.mp3` audio formats. The audio files should be recorded at 44.1 khz, 16 bit (the same as audio CDs). They can be either mono or stereo files.

See also

- The *Editing Audio* recipe in *Chapter 2, Create Your Course with Presenter*

Using Engage to create a glossary

Being able to create an interactive glossary in Engage is extremely useful. These glossaries can be used in Engage, and we can use them as a glossary for a presentation made in Articulate Presenter as well.

Items that are published into Presenter from Engage can either be published as a slide or as a tab on Presenter's Player. Glossaries created in Engage and then published as a tab in the Presenter Player can be made available to the viewers or learners throughout the entire presentation, facilitating their understanding.

Getting ready

We're going to create a new interaction. So the only preparation is to open Articulate Engage.

How to do it...

A glossary is a list of words with their definitions. So we will need to add the words we want to our glossary and then create definitions for them. To create a glossary using Engage perform the following steps:

1. From the Engage start screen, click on **Create a new interaction**. When the **New Interaction** dialog box opens, select the tab for **Glossary** and click on **OK**.

2. Title your glossary by typing its name in the textbox entitled **Interaction Title**.

3. The screen will open with three mock terms; you can edit these terms or add new ones, deleting the mock ones. To add a term, click on the **Add Entry** button in the lower-left corner of the screen or click on the **Add Entry** button on the ribbon in the **Glossary Entries** section.

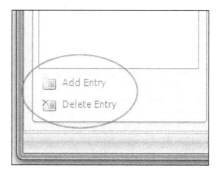

4. The central column of the screen is where the terms are defined. Type in the name of the term in the textbox labeled **Term**.

5. Type in the definition of the term in the larger textbox below the term. This can be fully formatted as in a word processor.

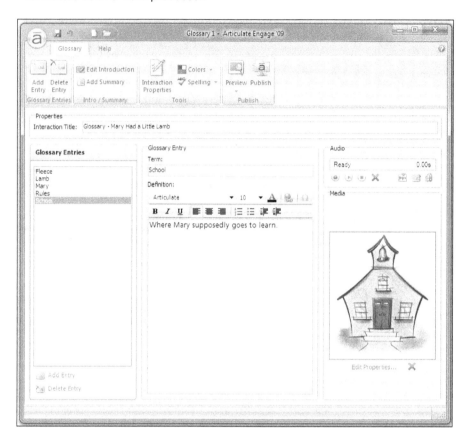

6. The terms will automatically be alphabetized in the left-hand side column.

7. You can add a picture for each entry in the glossary. This is done in the same way as adding pictures in any other interaction.

8. You can add audio to the glossary for each entry, making it an audible glossary. This is done in the same way as adding and editing audio to any other interaction.

9. You can delete the mock entries that were in the glossary when you opened it by selecting the entry and clicking on the **Delete Entry** button in the lower-left corner of the screen or by clicking on the **Delete Entry** button on the ribbon in the **Glossary Entries** section.

How it works...

Like the other Articulate products, Engage produces a Flash video file. This makes it fully compatible with the other programs in the Articulate suite.

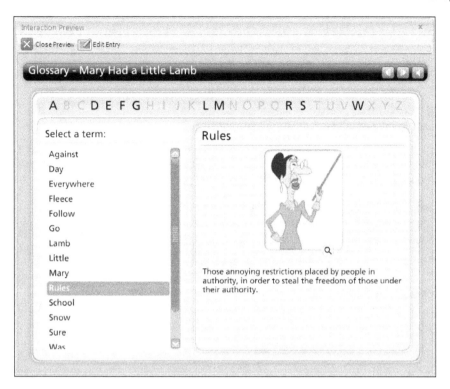

The finished glossary will need to be published from Engage. There is a line of the alphabet across the top of the glossary, allowing quick navigation for longer glossaries. The list of terms appears in the left-hand side column, with the definition and any media in the right-hand side column.

See also

- ▸ The *Adding images and video in Engage* recipe
- ▸ The *Adding and editing audio* recipe

Creating a labeled graphic

Labeled graphics are different from other types of interactions. With them you can label a diagram, providing information about its various parts. This can be very useful for a number of different things, such as identifying the parts of a machine, providing additional information about components, or highlighting the details of a photo with information.

Getting ready

This is a separate type of interaction, so you will not need to work from a previously created interaction. You will need to have Articulate Engage open.

How to do it...

We're going to need to start with the graphic that we want to use. Engage doesn't provide much editing capability for graphics, so you may need to edit it in a graphics program before importing it into Engage. To create a labeled graphic perform the following steps:

1. From the Engage start screen, click on the button that says **Create a new interaction**. When the **New Interaction** dialog box opens, select the **Labeled Graphic** tab and click on the **OK** button.

2. The interaction creation screen will open with a default image in the background. There is a button in the middle which allows you to change the image. You can also change the image at any time by clicking on the **Change Image...** button on the ribbon. Clicking on this button opens a standard, Windows open file dialog box where you can select the new image, as shown in the following screenshot:

3. By default, the interaction will open with four markers on the screen, one which is green and three that are red. These can be freely moved anywhere on the screen. To move them, click on the marker and then drag-and-drop them to its new location.

4. When you click on a marker, the label for that marker automatically appears beside it. To edit your labels, click on a label and then click on **Edit Labels** in the **Labels** section of the ribbon. This will open the **Edit Labels** dialog box, as shown in the following screenshot:

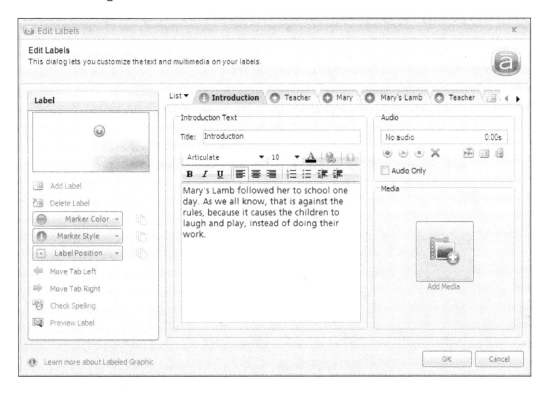

5. Each label has both a title and a description. These can be edited in the central portion of the dialog box. Simply click on the textbox and type.

6. Additional labels can be added to your graphic by either clicking on the **Add Label** tab (found to the far right of the tabs), or the **Add Label** button in the left-hand side pane of the dialog box.

7. The labels can also be customized as to their color, style, and position around the marker. There are standard colors and styles built into the program, which can be accessed by clicking on the appropriate button in the **Label** section of the dialog box.

8. Before publishing your interaction, spellcheck it. There are two places to do so, either with the **Spelling** button on the ribbon or with the **Check Spelling** button in the **Label** section of the **Edit Labels** dialog box.

9. To preview the interaction and verify that it will be published as you desire, click on the **Preview** button on the ribbon. It will take a couple of minutes for Engage to create the fully functional preview.

How it works...

The finished interaction will be published as a Flash video file. When viewed either on the Internet or in Presenter, the labels will be represented by the markers. The introduction label will be displayed. When the viewer hovers his/her mouse over a marker, the title of that marker will be displayed. Clicking on the marker will cause the text and media to be displayed.

In the following screenshot, I've clicked on the marker for the teacher to open the label fully and provide us with the additional information about the teacher and her official school photo:

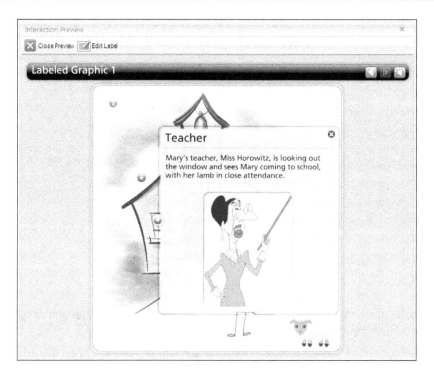

The label can be closed by clicking on the "**X**" button in the upper-right corner or by clicking elsewhere in the graphic.

There's more...

Images, video, and audio can be added to the labels on your interaction. See the sections on *Adding images and video in Engage* and *Adding and editing audio* in this chapter for more specific information on how to do this.

When adding video, it is important to ensure that the items that will have markers stay in one position on the video. The markers do not move, nor is there a time line capability to have them appear and disappear during the time when video is running.

See also

▸   The *Adding images and video in Engage* recipe
▸   The *Adding and editing audio* recipe

Previewing and publishing your interaction

As Articulate Engage produces a Flash video file, it is necessary to publish your interaction rather than use it in its raw form. This is a largely automatic process, performed by the program with a little input from you.

Getting ready

You'll need an interaction that is ready to publish. If you have been keeping the interaction that we've been working on in the last several recipes, you can use that. If not, you'll need to create a simple interaction. Any type of interaction will do, but it needs to have at least two steps.

How to do it...

There are two stages to this, first previewing the interaction to make sure that it is working the way that you want, and then publishing it. To preview and publish your interaction, perform the following steps:

1. Click on the **Preview** button on the ribbon. The program will generate your preview. This will take a couple of minutes. Don't worry if the status bar gets terminated and disappears, and the preview doesn't appear, as the program is still creating it.

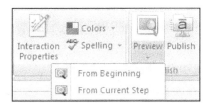

2. Cycle through the various steps of the preview to verify that it is working as you desire. If not, close the preview and return to the main Engage screen to make the changes. By using the **Edit Step** button in the preview, the program will take you directly to that step so that you can edit it.

3. Once you are satisfied with the interaction, click on the **Publish** button on the ribbon; this will open the **Publish** dialog box, as shown in the following screenshot:

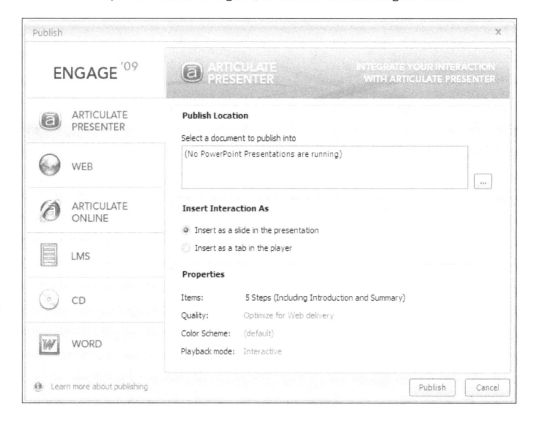

4. To publish to a presentation made in Articulate Presenter, you will need to select the presentation. If it is not currently open, you can select it by clicking on the **...** (ellipses) button to the right-hand side of the list of presentations.

5. Choose whether you want to have the presentation appear as a slide in the presentation or as a tab in the player. For most purposes, you will insert it as a slide in the presentation.

6. When you click on the **Publish** button, the program will create the Flash video file. This will take several minutes.

How it works...

Articulate Engage can be published in most of the same formats as Articulate Presenter. However, it is unable to be published to a podcast (audio file only). In order to use the interaction as a standalone presentation, you will want it to be published to the Web. This will not publish it to the Web, but instead will create a file on your computer with everything needed to publish it to the Web.

There are a number of interactions available for downloading on Articulate's website. They are located under **Downloads** in the **Community** section of the website. To find them, go to `Community.Articulate.com`. In the tabs at the top of the screen, select **Download**. From there you'll have to select **Articulate Engage** from the **E-Learning Templates** section.

There's more...

Articulate Engage can also publish the interaction directly, which is formatted for the Web or an LMS. These options are selected from the tabs on the **Publish** dialog box.

When publishing to an LMS, it is important to make sure that you check the type of LMS you are working with, in order for Engage to provide the learner's scores to the LMS in the correct format. Although the interactions created with Engage aren't typically graded as a quiz would be, you can ensure that the learner uses it by setting the number of items that the learner must view. To publish the presentation to an LMS perform the following steps:

1. To set the LMS options, click on the **Reporting and Tracking** button in the **LMS** tab of the **Publish** dialog box. This will open the **Reporting and Tracking Options** dialog box, as shown in the following screenshot:

2. Although the LMS format can be changed from the **Publish** dialog box, it can be done here as well.

3. You can see the title for your interaction here, along with a description and how much time in which the learner is allowed to complete it.

4. The very last item in the dialog box is the **Minimum number of items viewed to complete** checkbox. This can be set as any number, up to the maximum number of items that are included in the interaction.

Not all LMS reporting systems work in the same way. In order to use this function, you will need an understanding of your system's LMS reporting. If you are unsure about the proper settings to be used, check with your LMS administrator.

See also

▸ The *Previewing and publishing your course* recipe in *Chapter 3, Preparing Your Player*

7
Basic Video Editing with Video Encoder

In this chapter we will cover:

- ▶ Creating an FLV video for using in your course
- ▶ Cutting out a specific video segment
- ▶ Branding your video
- ▶ Editing audio in your video
- ▶ Creating your own webcam video
- ▶ Customizing your encoding settings

Introduction

Articulate can only work with videos that are compatible with Flash. Therefore, all other videos need to be converted to Flash before they can be used in Presenter, Quizmaker, or Engage. To facilitate this, the suite comes with a Video Encoder. This will convert standard video formats into the `.flv` format for using them with your Articulate presentations.

Clicking on the **Articulate Video Encoder** icon on your desktop or in your Windows Start menu will open up the Video Encoder startup screen. On this screen, you can select whether you open an existing video that is on your computer or record a video with your webcam. If you have recently used Video Encoder to work on other videos, they will show up on this screen as well, allowing you to select them.

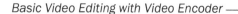

As with most video editing software, Video Encoder doesn't edit the video as you are making changes. Rather, it saves a series of instructions. Then, when you click on the **Publish** button, it does the actual edit, "rendering" the new video. This allows you to go back and modify a project if necessary.

The encoder provides some editing capability for your videos. However, this editing capability is somewhat limited. It allows you to trim, crop, add a watermark, and make some adjustments to your video quality. If you have major editing to do, such as multiple overlays and adding text, you will need to do that with a video editing program, before converting the video with Encoder.

Creating an FLV video for using in your course

There are some video formats that do not convert to `.flv`, while others do. So, even though they appear in the import video dialog box, that doesn't guarantee that your video will import well.

Getting ready

You'll need a short video that you can convert. Any of the standard video formats will work. The longer the video, the longer it will take to convert.

How to do it...

To create an FLV video perform the following steps:

1. When you open Video Encoder, the opening screen will provide you with three options—**Import a video file**, **Record your webcam**, or **Open a recent video**. We're going to select **Import a video file**. For simplicity sake, I'm going to use the wildlife sample video that comes with Windows.

2. Clicking on **Import a video file** will open a standard Windows open file dialog box. Locate the video you want to import, select it, and click on the **Open** button. This will automatically open the Video Encoder screen, as follows:

3. You can check your video by playing it right in the video encoder. Use the **Play** and **Stop** buttons (circled in the screenshot) to verify that you have the correct video and that it is functioning correctly.

4. Click on the **Publish** button on the ribbon to make Video Encoder convert the video. A **Publish** dialog box will open, allowing you to select the location and name of your encoded video. Clicking on the ellipsis button to the right of the **Folder** textbox allows you to search for the location.

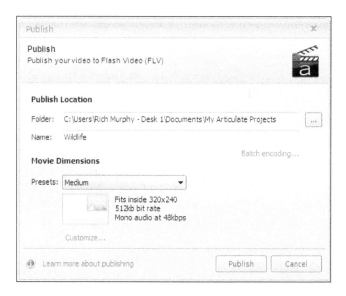

5. The default size for the video will be **Medium (320x240)** pixels. This is the most common video size used on the Web. YouTube videos that are not HD are of this size. You can change the video size to **Large (480x360)** or **Small (240x180)** by selecting the size in the **Presets** drop-down menu under **Movie Dimensions**.

6. Clicking on the **Publish** button in the dialog box causes the conversion process to begin. Please note that this process does take some minutes to complete. How long it actually takes will depend upon the length of your video.

How it works...

Video Encoder imports the specified file, usually a Windows Movie file (`.avi`, `.wmv`, `.wmf`), an MPEG format (`.mpg`, `.mp4`), or a QuickTime movie (`.mov`), and converts it to a Flash Video file format (`.flv`) so that it can be used in the Articulate suite programs.

There's more...

If you have a number of videos to convert, you can speed up the process by using batch encoding. You can't use this option if you are going to edit the videos, nor do you have the option to preview your videos before converting them. However, you don't have to select each video individually, and then wait for it to go through the conversion process.

Perform the following steps to use batch encoding:

1. Open a video to be converted it in Encoder. In the **Publish** dialog box, there is a legend in blue that says **Batch encoding...** Click on this to select the videos you will be converting.

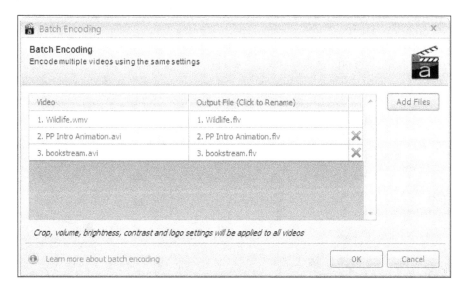

2. Add videos to the list to be converted by clicking on the **Add Files** button and locating the videos.

3. To convert the files, click on the **OK** button. All of the videos will be converted to the same settings as the original video that you had selected before clicking on batch convert.

Cutting out a specific video segment

Articulate Encoder has some video editing capability included in it. While it doesn't have the capability of stitching video segments together or adding text overlays, it does allow you to trim the video and crop it to zoom in only on a part of the frame.

Getting ready

You'll need to have Video Encoder open, with a video loaded that you can work with. I'm using the same video from the last recipe.

How to do it...

We're going to do both trimming and cropping in this recipe. Perform the following steps to do so:

1. Play the video through in its entirety, so that you know what it contains. You may want to take some notes of timestamps when events start and scenes change. You can find the time in the first column of the data in the lower-right corner of the screen. A red cursor line on the timeline lets you know where you are in the video as it plays.

2. Click on the **Trim** button on the ribbon. The timeline below the video image will change, adding gray bars at the beginning and end of the trimmed area, as shown in the following screenshot:

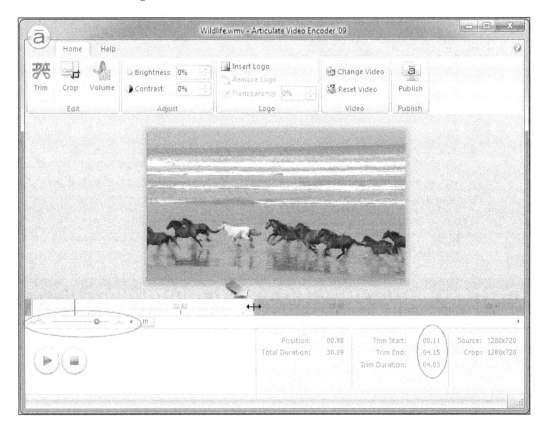

3. To adjust the trim point, move the end of the gray bars by dragging-and-dropping them to the new location. The video image will show the point in time that you are working at. The grayed-out areas in the timeline are the ones which will be trimmed off.

4. Note that the center column of figures in the data section of the screen changes to match your movement of the trim points.

5. If you need a finer time scale, use the slider below the timeline to adjust the scale of the timeline.

6. Click on the **Crop** button on the ribbon. This will create a highlighted rectangle on the video image. Once again, the grayed-out area is what will be eliminated.

7. You can adjust the size of the crop using the handles on the edge of the cropbox. The corner handles will maintain the aspect ratio, while the side ones will only stretch the image in that direction.

8. To see the results of your editing, you will need to click on the **Publish** button on the ribbon. This will create a new edited video as a `.flv` video file.

How it works...

The data area in the lower-right corner of the screen provides you with a lot of valuable information. It is divided into three columns. The first column tells you how long the original video is, along with the cursor position in seconds and hundredths of a second. The second column tells you about your trim information. The third tells you the original image size and the cropped image size. If you crop the video to the point where the cropped image size becomes smaller than the output size of your finished video, it will affect the image quality.

There's more...

Try not to crop the video smaller than the screen size for your selected output, as this will cause the video to become stretched and pixelated, and distortion will be introduced.

You can edit a video and return to the original one after you publish. When you want to re-edit a video and republish it, it might help to delete the file you have just created or rename it. The encoder will not overwrite the existing version.

Branding your video

Probably the most common way of branding commercial video is to add a logo or watermark to it. The difference is that the logo is at full image opacity, while the watermark has been made somewhat transparent.

Getting ready

You'll need Articulate Encoder open, with a video already imported into it. I'm using the same video that I used in the last recipe.

How to do it...

The procedure for adding a logo or watermark is the same. The only difference is in adding transparency for a watermark. Perform the following steps to brand your video:

1. Click on the **Insert Logo** button in the **Logo** section of the ribbon. This will open a Windows open file dialog box, where you can select the image you want to use. Click on the image, then click on the **Open** button.

2. Move the logo to the position where you want to have it on the video by clicking anywhere within the logo image and dragging it to the new location.

3. Resize the logo image by using the handles on its edges. If you use the corner handles, the image's aspect ratio will be maintained. If you use the side handles, the logo will be stretched:

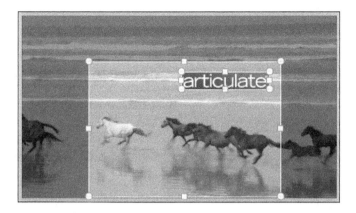

4. To convert the logo into a watermark, change the transparency. This is done by changing the percentage in the **Transparency** textbox in the **Logo** portion of the ribbon:

5. As you can see from the preceding example, about an 80 percent transparency produces a nice watermark, which isn't overpowering. A 50 percent transparency is much more obvious, but hides the image behind it a little too well.

How it works...

The logo or watermark will be added to your video when it is published. It will be a permanent part of this new video, not an overlay. Changing it later would require coming back into Encoder and recreating the edited video.

It is not necessary to save the changes you make in Encoder, as it automatically saves all changes. The next time you open the same video in Encoder, it will show you all of the same settings and edits that you have created.

There's more...

Although this feature is designed for adding a logo or watermark to a video, it can be used for any image overlay. With the same procedure, you can add a frame around the video. The only precaution for this is that the frame would have to have a transparent center to work. However, you can only add one image, so you couldn't add both a watermark and a frame.

Editing audio in your video

Video quality isn't just about the image that you see, but also about the quality of the audio track. The quality of the audio contained within a video can make otherwise wonderful video totally unusable. The two major problems that destroy video are background noise and low volume.

While it is almost impossible to do anything with background noise on an already recorded video, the volume level is something that's fairly easy to improve. Articulate Encoder includes the capability to adjust audio volume.

Getting ready

You'll need a video file open in Encoder. I'm using the same video that I've been using for the other recipes in this chapter.

How to do it...

To edit audio in your video perform the following steps:

1. Click on the **Volume** button in the **Edit** section of the ribbon. This will open the **Change Volume** dialog box, as shown in the following screenshot:

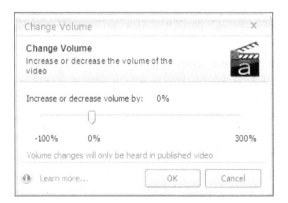

2. The dialog box only contains one control, a slider for adjusting the volume. It will be set at **0%** when the dialog box opens. To increase the volume, move the slider to the right-hand side by the amount you think is appropriate.

 The only way of checking the volume you've set is by publishing the video. The changes will not take effect until then.

How it works...

Although simple, this adjustment solves one of the most common problems with videos, that of the volume not being loud enough. Pretty much any video that is not commercially produced will need to be amplified to at least 200 percent (double the original volume level). You may have to experiment with volume levels a bit to get it right.

Be careful not to overamplify your audio. If the volume level gets too loud, the audio will start "clipping", a form of distortion where the tops of the wave peaks are cut off. You will notice that the audio will start to sound muddy and words won't be as easily discernible.

There's more...

See the *Editing audio in your video* recipe for more information about audio distortion and how to properly set the audio volume level.

Creating your own webcam video

It may turn out that you want to record your own video of yourself speaking, perhaps as an introduction to a training class, perhaps providing commentary about a product. Recording via webcam has become a very popular way of adding commentary, whether on YouTube or in your own production. Regardless of the reason for wanting a video of yourself to put into a presentation, Articulate Video Encoder provides a way of recording from your webcam and outputting it as an FLV encoded video for Flash.

Getting ready

You'll need Articulate Video Encoder open. Since we will be recording the video, you won't need to have a video open.

How to do it...

To create your own webcam video perform the following steps:

1. From the Encoder opening screen, click on **Record your webcam**. This will cause the **Record Webcam** dialog box to open.

 If you are already in Encoder and want to record, you can access **Record Webcam** from the round **Articulate** button in the upper-left corner of the screen.

2. If your webcam is not properly connected, or Encoder isn't receiving a signal from it, it will say **No Signal**. In this case, click on **More device settings**.

3. Click on the **Video Device** drop-down menu to select your webcam from available devices. Then click on the **OK** button.

4. To record, click on the round red **Record** button below the camera image. Be ready to start, as the recording will begin immediately.

5. When done recording, click on the **Stop** button, which has a square on it.

6. Play your recording to verify that it came out the way that you want (the **Record** button changes to a play button).

7. When you are satisfied with your recording, you can click on the **Save...** button.

How it works...

The Encoder records the video it captures from your webcam as a `.wmf` file. This allows you to edit it in the Encoder, applying all of the editing possibilities we've discussed in this chapter. Once you are done editing it, Encoder will save it to the `.flv` format when you publish.

There's more...

While any video can be used in an Articulate presentation, creating professional looking videos takes a little bit more effort. It is not necessary to have expensive equipment or a video studio to do this, you just need to use some basic good sense of videography. More than anything, good video comes from proper lighting.

A tripod is also very important. A handheld video tends to shake a lot, enough to be a distraction. Putting the camera on a tripod eliminates this, taking away a lot of the "amateur" quality of the video.

A word about lighting

Poor lighting will ruin otherwise good video. Many people don't have good lighting for their webcam. To rectify this, you'll need to have some lighting that's in front of you, off to the sides. Ideally, you want lighting on both sides, although it's best to have one stronger than the other. If you have a third light, it can be placed high, behind you, to light your hair. This provides a way for the camera to make your head look more three-dimensional, instead of flattening it out.

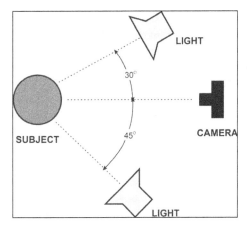

A word about audio

More good video has been ruined because of poor audio than any other reason. The microphone that's built into your webcam is not of a sufficiently high quality and it's too far away from your mouth; the result of this is that you'll end up sounding like you're in a tunnel. The easy solution is to buy a separate microphone and use this instead.

See also

- ▸ The *Cutting out a specific video segment* recipe
- ▸ The *Branding your video* recipe
- ▸ The *Editing audio in your video* recipe

Customizing your encoding settings

At times, you may find that the quality of your video or your needs in a presentation require some specialized tweaking of your video. Although Encoder is not a full video editing program, it does provide you with a number of things you can do, to customize the quality of your video according to your needs.

Getting ready

You'll need Encoder open, with a video already loaded. I'm using the same video that I've used for the rest of our editing.

How to do it...

While I have these written as a series of steps, each of them can be used individually. Perform the following steps:

1. The brightness and contrast of the video can be individually changed. They are changed using the **Brightness** and **Contrast** textboxes in the **Adjust** section of the ribbon. These settings are expressed as a percentage, as shown in the following screenshot:

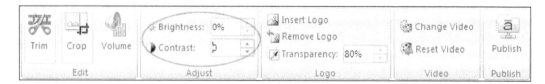

2. To darken the image instead of lightening it, use a negative percentage. Do the same to reduce the contrast in a video instead of increasing it. If you make a video brighter, you should also increase the contrast, to prevent it from appearing washed out:

3. To access the other customizable settings, click on the **Publish** button in the ribbon. In the **Publish** dialog box, find the legend, **Customize**, and click on it. This will open the **Custom Encoding** dialog box.

4. Changing the encoding method to **VBR (1 Pass)** or **VBR (2 Passes)** will improve video quality, but will also increase the time that the encoder takes to make the changes and the file size (more for two passes than for one pass).

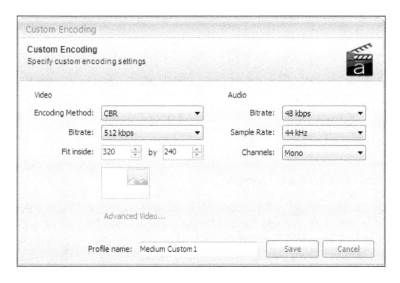

5. Changing the **Bitrate** setting will affect the quality of the video, but it will also affect the file size. The default bitrate is **512 kbps** for video and **44 kHz** for audio. Higher bitrates provide a better quality.

6. The settings under the **Advanced Video...** legend are for use with poor-quality video. The **Noise Reduction** feature is useful, especially if your video has static noise on it. Clicking on the drop-down menu allows you to select **Light** or **Heavy** noise reduction, as shown in the following screenshot:

7. To save your changes from any of these dialog boxes, click on the **OK** button.

How it works...

The video and audio bitrates can be set separately but they are merged together in the original video and in the published version.

If you do change these settings and you like their results, you should fill in the **Profile Name** field and save the profile so that you can apply it to other videos of the same quality.

The changes done in the **Publish** or **Custom Encoding** dialog box will not show up until the video is Encoded. There is no way to preview their effect.

8
Combining All Three

In this chapter we will cover:

- ▸ Adding a quiz to Presenter
- ▸ Adding an interaction to Presenter
- ▸ Using hyperlinks and branching to create a story
- ▸ Adding screencasts to your project
- ▸ Placing a glossary in the tab area
- ▸ Adding video to the logo and presenter panels
- ▸ Creating consistency when combining everything
- ▸ Getting a new wardrobe
- ▸ Creating special images or video questions in Quizmaker

Introduction

Although each of the products in the Articulate suite are capable of working independently, their real strength shows when they are used together. In this chapter, we're going to explore various ways to use the three together, drawing from the strengths of each.

When using these products together, the core product is Presenter. Quizzes created in Quizmaker and interactions created in Engage are designed to be inserted into presentations, providing a complete learning experience.

There are two ways to insert a Quizmaker or Engage file into the presentation. They can be generated from the buttons on the **Articulate** ribbon, which will cause them to be automatically inserted after the current slide, or they can be created separately and then inserted into the current open presentation.

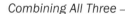

All quizzes and interactions take up a full slide in Presenter; they cannot be combined with other items on the same slide. To help maintain image consistency, the same color schemes can be used in all three packages. Engage and Quizmaker can also produce their outputs with transparent frames, allowing the background from the presentation to show through.

Adding a quiz to Presenter

Although Quizmaker is perfectly capable of working as an independent software package, which can create its own Flash presentations, it's mainly intended to create quizzes to be used together with Presenter. The two packages together can create a better overall program than either one by itself.

Getting ready

You'll need a presentation with at least one slide and a quiz with at least one question already created. If you have been saving any of your work from previous recipes, you can use a presentation and quiz from them.

We're going to be working from within Presenter, so you'll need Presenter open on your computer.

How to do it...

Inserting a quiz created in Quizmaker into a presentation in Articulate Presenter allows the creation of a complete independent study class, where the learner studies the material, and then immediately tests it. To add a quiz to Presenter perform the following steps:

1. From the **Articulate** ribbon in PowerPoint, click on the **Quizmaker Quiz** button in the **Insert** section of the ribbon. This will open the **Quizzes and Interactions** dialog box, as shown in the following screenshot:

2. Click on the **Quizmaker Quizzes** tab. In the top of the dialog box there is a textbox, which lists any quizzes you currently have in that presentation. Since we haven't added any quizzes yet, this box will be blank.

3. Click on the **Add Existing...** button. This will open a Windows open file dialog box, where you can select the quiz to be inserted in your presentation. Once you have selected it, click on the **Open** button.

4. You will now see an extra slide added to your presentation thumbnails, representing the quiz. It will also be listed in the textbox (the thumbnail may not be visible until after closing the dialog box). After the name of the slide will be the legend (slide x), where x represents the slide number in your slide order.

5. In the lower part of the dialog box there are a number of settings for how the quiz interacts with the presentation. The default setting can be changed to a number of others, available on the pull-down menus.

6. Click on the **Close** button to insert the quiz into the presentation.

7. The thumbnail slide of the quiz works just like the other thumbnails in the presentation. You can move it within the presentation by dragging-and-dropping it within the thumbnail pane on the left-hand side of PowerPoint.

How it works...

You can include multiple quizzes in the same presentation. Presenter accesses the completed quizzes and inserts them into the presentation at the appropriate point, merging the presentation and quiz into one Flash presentation.

Although you can't edit the quiz slides directly from within PowerPoint, you can always edit them in Quizmaker, up until the time you publish the presentation within Quizmaker. If you make a change after the presentation has been published, it will need to be republished.

There's more...

Although we worked with a pre-created quiz, it really doesn't have to be done that way. The Articulate suite allows you to work back and forth between the various programs, changing whatever you need, right up to the time of publication.

Editing a quiz

If you realize that there is something wrong with your quiz, you can edit it either by opening the Quizmaker program or by clicking on the **Edit quiz in Articulate Quizmaker** button. This will open the quiz slide, so that you can view and edit it. Perform the following steps:

1. Clicking the **Properties** button in the quiz slide overlay reopens the **Quizzes and Interactions** dialog box so that you can change properties.

2. Clicking on the **Edit quiz in Articulate Quizmaker** button in the quiz slide overlay opens Quizmaker to the main screen, where you can edit your quiz.

Creating a quiz

If you haven't already created your quiz ready to be imported to your presentation, you can launch Quizmaker directly from the **Quizzes and Interactions** dialog box. To do so, click on the **Create New...** button.

Although Quizmaker will open and operate normally, there is one change. The **Publish** button will be replaced by one that says **Save and Return to Presenter**. The Quizmaker file will automatically be inserted after the current Presenter slide.

See also

▶   *Chapter 3, Preparing Your Player*

▶   *Chapter 4, Creating Assessments and Courses with Quizmaker*

Adding an interaction to Presenter

Articulate Engage has been created to produce interactions that can be inserted into presentations made with Presenter. The interactions made in Engage can be used as standalone items, such as an individual glossary file. However, these same interactions provide a nice enhancement to presentations.

The Articulate suite allows you the flexibility to create an interaction in Engage and then import it into Presenter, or open Engage from within Presenter, in order to create your interaction.

Getting ready

You'll need a presentation with at least one slide and an interaction already created. If you have been saving any of your work from previous recipes, you can use a presentation and interaction from them.

We're going to be working from within Presenter, so you'll need Presenter open on your computer.

How to do it...

Just as we added a quiz to the presentation in the last recipe, we're going to add an interaction in this recipe. The steps are essentially the same, as follows:

1.   From the **Articulate** ribbon in PowerPoint, click on the **Engage Interaction** button in the **Insert** section of the ribbon. This will open the **Quizzes and Interactions** dialog box, as shown in the following screenshot:

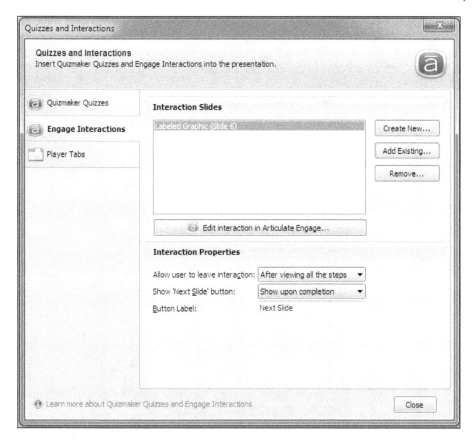

2. If it is not already open, click on the **Engage Interactions** tab. In the top of the dialog box there is a textbox, which lists any interactions you currently have in that presentation. If you haven't added any yet, this box will be blank.

3. Click on the **Add Existing...** button. This will open a Windows open file dialog box, where you can select the interaction to be inserted in your presentation. Once you have selected it, click on the **Open** button.

4. You will now see an extra slide added to your presentation thumbnails, representing the interaction. It will also be listed in the textbox (the thumbnail image may not be visible until after closing the dialog box). After the name of the slide will be the legend (slide x), where x represents the slide number in your slide order.

5. In the lower part of the dialog box there are a number of settings for how the interaction works with the presentation. The default setting can be changed to a number of others, available on the pull-down menus.

6. Click on the **Close** button to insert the interaction into the presentation.

7. The thumbnail slide of the interaction works just like the other thumbnails in the presentation. You can move it within the presentation by dragging-and-dropping it within the thumbnail pane to the left-hand side of PowerPoint.

How it works...

You can include multiple interactions and quizzes in the same presentation. Presenter accesses the completed interactions and inserts them into the presentation at the appropriate point, merging the presentation and interactions into a Flash presentation.

Although you can't edit the interaction slides directly from within PowerPoint, you can always edit the interactions up until the time you publish the presentation by accessing Engage. If you make a change after the presentation has been published, it will need to be published again.

There's more...

The Articulate suite allows the user flexibility in his/her working style. Although we worked with an already created interaction, Engage can be launched from within Presenter which allows you to create and edit the interactions.

Editing an interaction

If you realize that there is something wrong with your interaction, you can edit it either by opening the Engage application in the normal manner or by clicking on the **Edit interaction in Articulate Engage** button in the **Quizzes and Interactions** dialog box. This will open the interaction slide so that you can view it. Perform the following steps:

1. Clicking the **Properties** button in the interaction slide overlay reopens the **Quizzes and Interactions** dialog box so that you can change properties.

2. Clicking on the **Edit interaction in Articulate Engage** button in the quiz slide overlay opens Engage to the main screen, where you can make changes to your Interaction.

Creating an interaction

If you haven't already created your interaction ready to be imported to your presentation, you can launch Engage directly from the **Quizzes and Interactions** dialog box. To do so click the **Create New...** button.

Although Engage will open and operate normally, there is one change. The **Publish** button will be replaced by one that says **Save and Return to Presenter**. The Engage interaction will be inserted as the next slide, directly after the currently active slide in Presenter.

See also

   ▸   *Chapter 5, Taking Your Quiz to the Next Level*

   ▸   *Chapter 6, Creating Interactive Content with Engage*

Using hyperlinks and branching to create a story

There might be times when you want to have a simple quiz contained within a presentation, but not want to use Quizmaker or the Learning Games included within Articulate. One reason for this might be to maintain the same style as the rest of the presentation. Another reason might be if you are asking them a question to get them to think about the information being presented, but don't need the capability to grade their answer.

You can also use this same methodology to allow viewers to select what part of a presentation they are going to view. The same sales presentation could have a section that focuses on product features for the average audience, along with a more technical section for engineers. Branching the presentation allows the viewer to see only that part of the presentation which matters to them.

Branching allows the developer to create multiple tracks for the viewer. This is useful in a number of ways. When used for educational purposes, a track can be created to review a concept which has been evaluated through a quiz. Only those learners who don't pass the quiz would be taken to the track. When using Articulate Presenter to create sales or informative presentations, branching allows the developer to customize the viewer's experience, based upon his/her need.

One way to do this is by using branching to include a menu, where the viewer selects from a number of icons that direct him/her to different paths. A modification of this idea would be to allow the viewer to see product features or technical specifications. Branching allows the presentation developer to create the same sort of experience in a presentation that exists on the Web, allowing a viewer to choose what he/she will see next.

Getting ready

You'll need PowerPoint open, with the Articulate suite installed.

How to do it...

Hyperlinks are used in Presenter to create branching. They allow you great flexibility in how you set up your presentation. Depending upon your imagination, each viewer can literally be taken on a different path through the presentation. To use hyperlinks and branching perform the following steps:

1. Create a slide with a question on it. This will require putting in a textbox to contain the question. For the purpose of this recipe, we want to use a multiple-choice question, where the answers can be represented by pictures.

2. Add three pictures for the possible answers. To check the size of a picture, right-click on it, and select **Size and Position...** from the context sensitive menu.

3. Align the images by selecting them all, then clicking on the **Align** legend in the **Arrange** section of the **Format** ribbon. This will open a drop-down menu, where you can select how you want the pictures aligned. Since our pictures are placed in a row, it would be best to align them to the bottom of the image, as shown in the following screenshot;

4. In the PowerPoint pane on the left-hand side, right-click on the thumbnail of the slide and select **Copy** from the context sensitive menu. Then right-click below the slide and select **Paste** from the context sensitive menu. Repeat this twice, so that you have three copies of the slide.

5. In slide 2, click on and delete the images for the second and third answers. In slide 3, click on and delete the images for the first and third answers. In slide 4, click on and delete the first two answers.

6. Add a textbox to the bottom of slides 2, 3, and 4. In it type in `You're right` or `Wrong guess`, as appropriate.

7. Return to slide 1. Click on the first "answer" image. Then click on The **Hyperlink** button in the **Insert** ribbon. In the dialog box, select **Place in This Document** from the choices available on the left-hand side. This will show you a list of slides in the left-hand side textbox. Select **Slide 2** from the list. A thumbnail of the slide should show up to the right of the textbox. Verify that the image shown in the thumbnail is the correct slide. If so, click on the **OK** button:

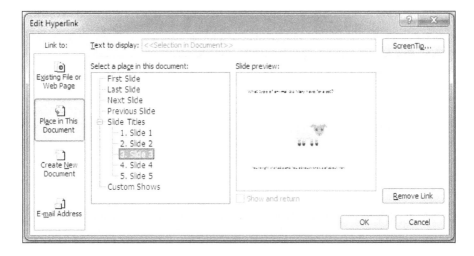

8. Repeat step 7 for the other two choices, linking them to slides 3 and 4.

9. Add a fifth slide to the presentation. Add a textbox with a legend, such as `Thanks for answering my question`.

10. In the **Articulate** ribbon, click on the **Slide Properties** button to open the **Slide Properties** dialog box.

11. In the **Slide Properties** dialog box, the right-hand side column is labeled **Advance**. This is used to tell the program how the presentation should advance to the next slide. There are two options—**Automatically** and **By User**. Click on each box, and change it to **By User**, as shown in the following screenshot:

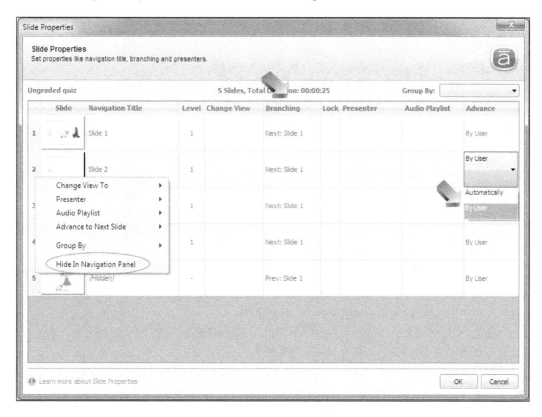

12. For slides 2 through 5, right-click on the slide numbers, which are listed all the way to the left-hand side of the dialog box. In the context sensitive menu that pops up, select **Hide In Navigation Panel**. You will see **Navigation Title** of these slides changed to read **(Hidden)**. Doing this will prevent the viewers from being able to see these slides in the list of slides, once the presentation is published.

13. In the **Branching** column, change the settings for **Slide 1** so that the **At end of slide, branch to** setting reads **Slide 1**. Leave **Previous button branches to** set to **(default)**, as shown in the following screenshot:

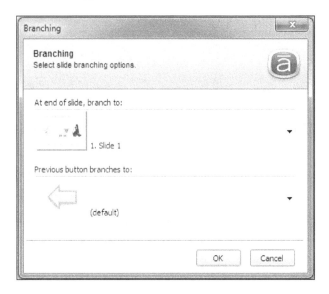

14. Branch slides 2, 3, and 4 so that the **At end of slide, branch to** setting reads **Slide 5** and **Previous button branches to** reads **Slide 1**.

15. Branch slide 5 so that the **Previous button branches to** setting reads **Slide 1**. Leave **At end of slide, branch to** set to **(default)**.

 There's a bug in Articulate Studio 09 where hyperlinks may not work properly in the preview mode. However, they will still work when published. If your hyperlinks don't work in preview, try publishing the presentation to check them.

How it works...

What we've just done is called **branching**. It allows the viewer to go to a number of different places from one slide, instead of just following the slides through their numbered sequence. This can be useful in a number of different applications, from training courses to sales presentations.

One way that this would be useful is for an online catalog. If a company is showing three different versions of their equipment, using this same method could take them to each of three different sections, which present the different models. At the end, they could be returned back to the choices menu or taken to a sales area.

The settings we made in the **Slide Properties** dialog box allow full control of the way that the viewer sees the branched part of the presentation. Without this, clicking on **Previous slide** would take the viewer back to the previous slide in the presentation, not skipping over the slides for the other answers. Likewise, setting the next slide that the viewer goes to, ensures that he/she doesn't see information that isn't appropriate to the branch that has been entered.

There's more...

To save time in future presentations, once you have created this type of branched presentation, you can use it as a template. Just copy and paste the slides into the new presentation. All the settings and hyperlinks will be copied over as well. By changing the images rather than deleting them, the hyperlinks will remain intact.

To change the images, click on the image you wish to change. In the **Format** ribbon, click on the **Change Picture** button. This will open a Windows open file dialog box, where you can select the new image. It will be imported into the slide at the same size and position as the old image.

Adding screencasts to your project

Screencasts are a very useful way to show an example of how to do anything on a computer. The screencast software captures everything that is happening on your computer screen, including the movement of your mouse cursor, and records it as a video.

Although Articulate suite doesn't have any screen capture capability, there is an application available online. This application, called Screenr, allows you to capture screencasts of up to 5 minutes and save them as videos. Those videos can then be downloaded and used in the various programs that are part of the Articulate suite.

 There are other commercially available screencast capture programs online, such as Camtasia and Snagit. They are used in pretty much the same way as Articulate Screenr.

Getting ready

Articulate's screen capture software is located on its own website at `www.screenr.com`. You'll want to open the website and sign in. In the upper-right corner of the screen, there's a button for signing in with your favorite e-mail or social networking site's login ID and password. Although only four icons are shown, you can sign in with:

- Facebook
- Twitter
- Google
- Yahoo

- ▸ LinkedIn
- ▸ Windows Live

Clicking on this button opens a small dialog box, where you can select which of these online services you want to use for signing in. Once selected, another dialog box opens, allowing you to input your ID and password. Clicking on **Sign In** completes the process and takes you back to the original screen.

Before starting to record your screencast, it's a good idea to have your script ready. While there are some people who can speak consistently effectively, the rest of us spend more time saying "uhh" than we do in saying anything effective.

How to do it...

Screencasts are created separately from the Articulate suite, and then imported as video into the presentation, quiz, or interaction. To add a screencast to your project perform the following steps:

1. Click on the yellow button on the Screenr website, which says **Launch screen recorder now!** It will take a moment for Screenr to open, as it needs to check the status of several things.

2. When Screenr opens on your computer screen, it will show a dotted line, to outline the area of the screen capture, along with a toolbar below it and a panel with instructions on how to use Screenr, as shown in the following screenshot:

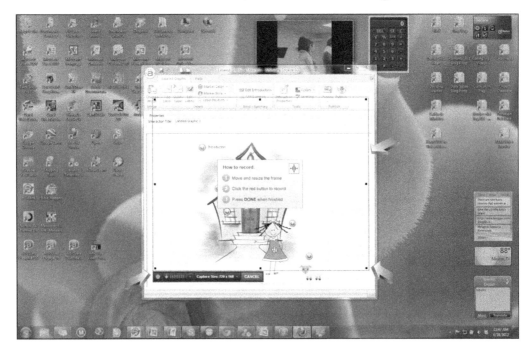

If you are using more than one monitor on your computer, Screenr will only operate on your main monitor.

3. Move the outline by clicking anywhere along the dotted line's border and dragging it to the new location.

4. Resize the Screenr outline to match the screen capture you want to do. The easiest way to do this is by using the eight handles on the corners and edges of the outline. Using the corner handles provides a proportional resize, while using the side, top, and bottom handles allows you to resize disproportionally.

5. Click on the red **Record** button on the capture toolbar to begin recording. The button will change to a **Pause** button. Screenr will give you a countdown, telling you when to start.

6. As you are completing the task that you want to capture, you can narrate it with your computer's microphone. There is a ribbon for VU meter in the toolbar to give you an idea of the volume of your narration. The counter will also let you know how much time you have left for your screencast recording.

7. If you need to stop in the middle of your screencast, click on the **Pause** button. It will change back to a **Record** button. Clicking on it again will continue your recording.

8. When done with your recording, click on the **DONE** button.

9. Your screencast will be loaded onto the Screenr web page for you to review. You can play the screencast, using the **Play** button below it:

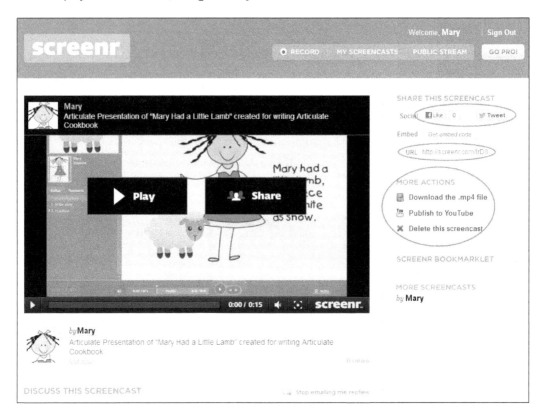

10. Provide an interesting description of your screencast for others who may view it.

11. Click on the **Publish** button. This will save your screencast on the Screenr website.

12. Download your screencast, using the **Download the .mp4 file** button on the right-hand side of the screen. It can then be used with Presenter, Engage, or Quizmaker.

How it works...

Screenr uses Java scripting to function. If you don't have Java installed on your computer, it won't run. As part of the startup process, the Screenr checks for the presence and function of Java on your computer.

There may be times when Screenr tells you that Java is not installed on your computer, even though it is. That could happen because Java isn't enabled. It could also happen if Screenr isn't recognizing Java as working with your browser; some browsers are better than others for this. If Java is installed and enabled, try using a different browser.

A good-quality microphone will make a difference in the quality of your screencast. If your webcam has an internal microphone, the distance between the webcam and your mouth will make it sound like you are in a tunnel. You can rectify this problem by moving the webcam about 6 inches away from your mouth.

There's more...

Screenr will also publish your screencast directly to YouTube, allow you to share it on Facebook, or mention it on Twitter. Since the video is saved online, it can be used in the same way as any other online video. The URL for your video will show up both in your browser's navigation panel and to the right-hand side of the video on the Screenr web page.

You can also resize the screen capture to exactly match the exact proportions of video. To do so click on the **Capture Size** legend in Screenr's toolbar. This will open a drop-down menu, where you can select the screen capture size you want, as shown in the following screenshot:

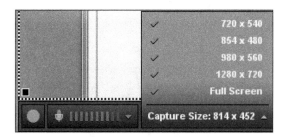

Editing your video

Although Screenr doesn't have any video editing capability, you can do some limited editing of your video in Articulate Video Encoder. If you need to do a more complicated edit of your video, you will need other video editing software.

Adding overlays to your video

Articulate Presenter doesn't allow adding overlays to a video, as the video is always on top of the stack. However you can still add overlays by putting the video into Quizmaker. Perform the following steps to do so:

1. Create a blank hotspot question in Quizmaker. Go to **Slide View** in the question editor.
2. Add the video by clicking on the **Flash Movie** button on the **Insert** ribbon.
3. Resize the video to fill the entire slide.

4. Overlay text, objects, and pictures on the video, as follows:

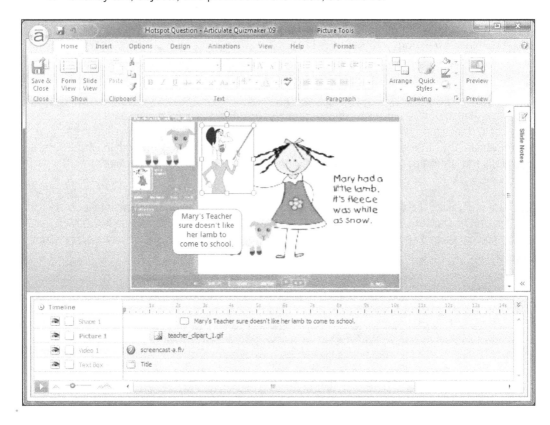

5. Adjust the timing of the overlay objects appearing in the **Timeline** section.

6. Publish your video as a quiz. It can then be inserted into Presenter, with the overlays being intact.

See also

▶ The *Adding images to a slide* recipe in *Chapter 4, Creating Assessments and Courses with Quizmaker*

Placing a glossary in the tab area

Glossaries can be very useful to the viewer or learner, especially if your presentation is covering complex material. Many projects include technical jargon which is not widely understood. Adding a glossary can clarify the definitions of these words for viewers, making your presentation much more viewer friendly.

Getting ready

Glossaries are prepared in Articulate Engage. To be able to add a glossary to a presentation, you will also need to have a presentation ready and open.

Before adding your glossary, it's a good idea to already have a list of words that you are planning to use, along with their definitions and any images you wish to include.

How to do it...

To add the glossary, we're going to use both Engage and Presenter. The glossary will be created in Engage, and then imported into Presenter. However, it won't be imported in the same way that we've imported other interactions. To place a glossary, perform the following steps:

1. There is no button on the **Articulate** ribbon in PowerPoint for adding a glossary to the presentation. However, it can be added as a tab and made available throughout the entire presentation by clicking on the **Engage Interaction** button on the ribbon.

2. Select the **Player Tabs** tab in the dialog box.

3. Click on the **Add Existing...** button in the dialog box. This will open a Windows open file dialog box, where you can select the glossary for your presentation. After selecting it, click on the **Open** button.

4. The name of the glossary will now show up in the textbox in the center of the dialog box, as follows:

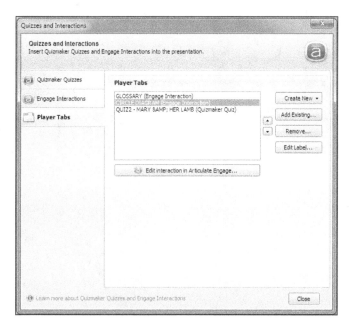

5. Click on the **Edit Label...** button. This will allow you to change the name of the glossary from the filename to one that is more appropriate for your presentation. Remember, a short name is better, as it needs to fit into the tab.

How it works...

Unlike adding a quiz or interaction to the presentation, there won't be any marker slide added into the presentation. As the glossary is being added to a tab in the presenter, rather than the presentation itself, it won't show up until the presentation is previewed or published.

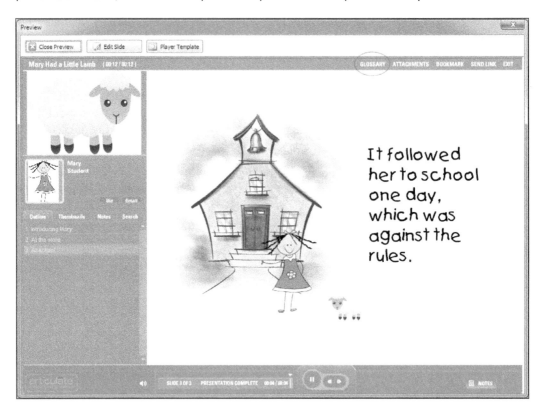

Whenever the **GLOSSARY** tab is clicked in the presentation player, the glossary will open, allowing the viewer to interact with it. The player will be paused while the glossary is being used, and then restarted once the glossary is closed.

There's more...

Although we've used this procedure to put a glossary as a tab in the presenter, the same thing can be done with any interaction made in Engage or any quiz made in Quizmaker. The number of tabs you can add is limited by the amount of space in the tab bar.

See also

> ▸ The *Using Engage to create a glossary* recipe in *Chapter 6, Creating Interactive Content with Engage*

Adding video to the logo and presenter panels

One option for creating a company brand with more impact is to use videos for your company logo and the presenter. These are added in essentially the same way as the images.

Getting ready

We'll be working in PowerPoint, so we'll need it open with a presentation of at least one slide.

How to do it...

Adding a logo to your presentation helps you promote your company. Having an animated logo is even better, as it is more eye-catching to the viewer. Perform the following steps to add video to the logo and presenter panels:

1. Click on the **Presentation Options** button in the **Articulate** ribbon. Click on the **Logos** tab in the dialog box, as shown in the following screenshot:

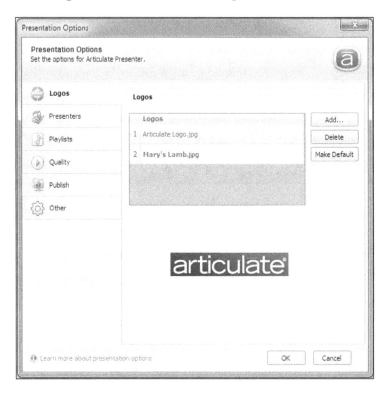

2. Click on the **Add...** button to select the video and add it to the Logo library. This will open a Windows open file dialog box, where you can select the video to use. Once selected, click on the **Open** button.

The video must be in the .swf format to be used as the logo. It is recommended that the video should not be more than 244 pixels wide, as this is the width of the area for the logo in the sidebar.

3. The name of the video will now appear in the list of logos in the dialog box.

4. Click on **OK** to close the **Presentation Options** dialog box.

5. Click on the **Flash Movie** legend in the **Insert** section of the **Articulate** ribbon. This will open a Windows open file dialog box. Once you select the video of the presenter, click on the **Open** button.

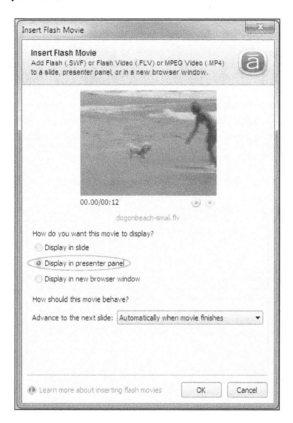

6. The **Insert Flash Movie** dialog box will open. Below the thumbnail of the video, the dialog box asks the question, **How do you want this movie to display?** Select the radio button for **Display in presenter panel**, as shown in the preceding screenshot.

How it works...

When you publish the presentation, Presenter will insert the videos into the presenter side panel in place of the images for the logo and presenter. Please note that this may affect the performance of the presentation, especially when used over the Internet in locations where a high-speed presentation is not available. If the presentation is to be used in places where a high-speed Internet connection is not available, it is not advisable to use videos in the presenter panel.

See also

▶ The *Adding your company's logo* recipe in *Chapter 3, Preparing Your Player*

▶ The *Setting up a player template* recipe in *Chapter 3, Preparing Your Player*

Creating consistency when combining everything

As you've probably noticed, Quizmaker and Engage don't look anything like Presenter. Unfortunately, that makes it a bit tricky to brand your presentation when combining all three products in the Articulate suite. However, there are some things you can do to make it run a little smoother.

One of the signature styling elements of PowerPoint, which is used in Presenter, is the ability to have multicolored backgrounds and background images. While this can't be carried over into Quizmaker and Engage, the frames for slides created in these two products can be made transparent, allowing those backgrounds to show through. This provides some visual continuity between Presenter and the other Articulate products.

Getting ready

Since we're going to be working in all three Articulate products, we'll need them all open. You will also need presentations that are already prepared in all three.

How to do it...

We're going to start by working in Quizmaker; the procedure for Engage is almost the same. Perform the following steps:

1. To start with, we need to tell Presenter that we will be using transparent frames in Quizmaker and Engage. Click on the **Presentation Options** button on the **Articulate** ribbon.

2. In the **Presentation Options** dialog box, select the **Publish** tab. Click on the checkbox that says **Include slide master behind quizzes and interactions**. Then click on the **OK** button:

3. In Quizmaker, select the **Player Templates** button from the ribbon in the main window.

4. Select a template in the dialog box and click on the **Edit** button.

5. In the **Player Template Builder** dialog box, select the **Colors and Effects** tab.

6. In the top of the dialog box, there is a dropbox for selecting the color scheme to use. Select the color scheme that you are going to use as a base, and then click on the **Edit** button to the right-hand side of the color scheme.

7. If we make it too transparent, we're not going to be able to see the slide well; so all we're going to make transparent is the frame. In the bottom of the **Color Scheme Editor** window, there is a dropbox, which is labeled **Choose an item to edit**. Select **Frame**, then in the fly-out menu, select **Outer Border**.

8. To the right-hand side of the dropbox, there is a textbox labeled **Transparency**. Type in `100%` in this box, as shown in the following screenshot:

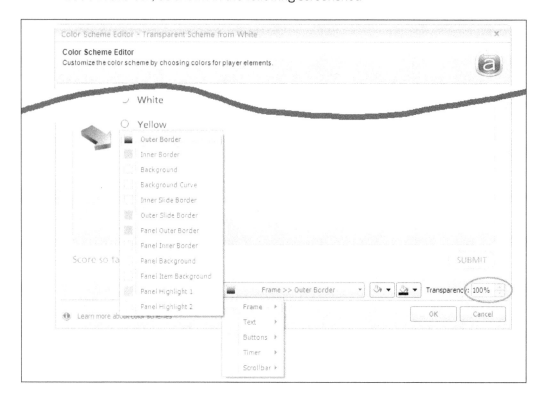

9. Repeat steps 7 and 8 with selecting **Frame | Inner Border** and **Frame | Background**, as well.

10. Click on the **OK** button. The program will ask you if you want to change the new color scheme.

11. Click on the **OK** button in the **Player Template Builder** dialog box; it will ask you for a new name for the color scheme.

How it works...

When you insert the Quizmaker quiz into the presentation, the frame on the quiz will be transparent allowing the same background style that you used in Presenter to show through. This will help to maintain the image consistency. Although you won't actually see the changes in Quizmaker, you will see them once you pull the quiz into Presenter.

To further the effect, you can apply the same color scheme and lettering style that you used in Presenter to your Quizmaker quiz or Engage interaction.

There's more...

We've just created a transparent frame in Quizmaker; now let's do the same thing for an interaction created in Engage. We won't be able to make it quite as transparent, but we can still create the same effects.

Creating transparent frames in Engage

Creating transparent frames in Engage is almost identical to creating them in Quizmaker, with some exceptions. Perform the following steps:

1. To open the **Color Scheme Editor** window, click on the **Colors** button in the **Tools** section of the ribbon. When the drop-down menu appears, select **New Color Scheme** from the bottom of the menu, as shown in the following screenshot:

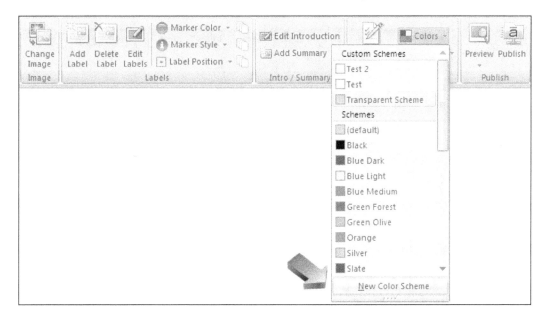

2. In the **Color Scheme Editor** window, the only thing you want to change to transparent is the background. The procedure for changing it is the same as in Quizmaker.

3. Once you are done changing the background to transparent, click on the **OK** button to close the editor and save your changes.

See also

▶ The *Modifying slide masters* recipe in *Chapter 1, Getting Started with Articulate Suite*

▶ The *Creating a branched story* recipe in *Chapter 5, Taking Your Quiz to the Next Level*

Getting a new wardrobe

We've already discussed creating templates and customizing the Flash video player in *Chapter 3, Preparing Your Player*. There's a bit more that can be done. Here we're going to put a new skin on the player, modifying the look and not just the color. These are third-party Flash customizations that are available for download from the Articulate website.

How to do it...

Changing skins on an Articulate presentation can help you make it more customized and improve company branding. A number of privately created skins are available for this. Perform the following steps:

1. Access the new skins on the following Articulate website:

   Community.Articulate.com

2. In the tabs at the top of the web page, click on **Downloads**.

3. The new page will have a number of icons for the available templates and other aids. Click on the icon that says **Articulate Presenter**, as shown in the following screenshot:

4. This opens a page that has the new skins on it. To download any of them, click on the thumbnail. This will open a page specific to that skin, where you can download it.

5. The skins get downloaded as package files (`.pkg`). To install them, simply click on the file; it will install automatically.

6. You do not need to access the skin until you are ready to publish your presentation. Clicking on the **Publish** button in the **Articulate** ribbon opens the **Publish** dialog box, as follows:

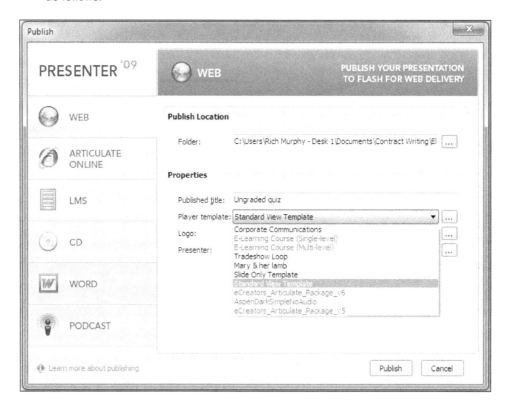

7. Select the new skin from the **Player template** drop-down menu in the dialog box (the items highlighted in yellow in the preceding screenshot are templates).

8. When you publish the presentation, the skin will automatically be substituted for the standard skin.

How it works...

These skins are Flash customizations, so you won't see the changes that the skins make until publishing.

There's more...

Although the skins are a modification to the presenter that are already done and packaged, they can still be customized in the same way as the standard skin. For details on how to customize the skin, see the *Setting up a player template* recipe in *Chapter 3, Preparing Your Player*.

See also

▶ The *Setting up a player template* recipe in *Chapter 3, Preparing Your Player*

Creating special images or video questions in Quizmaker

At times, it might be useful to have the capability to overlay text, images, and objects over an existing Flash video or animation created in Presenter. However, Presenter does not allow anything to be overlaid onto videos, always keeping the video on the top of the stack of objects on a slide.

This doesn't mean that it can't be done though. Quizmaker allows placement of objects over videos which can then be published as new videos and brought into Presenter.

Another way that this can be done is to take a video from an existing presentation and overlay new information and graphics onto it. When the presentation is published, each slide becomes its own Flash video. These can then be imported into future presentations or into Quizmaker, where they can have text, images, and shapes overlaid on them.

Getting ready

You'll need a video that you can use. If you've published a presentation in Presenter, you can look at the folder that contains the presentation slides. The slides of that presentation will be titled **slide1.swf**, **slide2.swf**, and so on, as shown in the following screenshot:

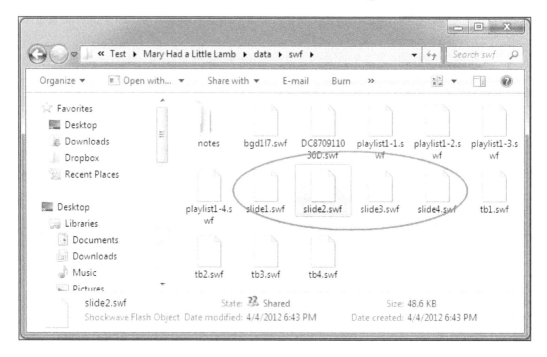

We're going to work in Quizmaker, so you will need it open.

How to do it...

Although we're going to be working with an already created video, there are times where more information might need to be added. This will allow us to modify that video for use in another presentation. To create special images or video questions perform the following steps:

1. Select a new graded or survey question in Quizmaker. You can use any type of question for overlaying it onto your video. Remember that the question and answer spaces will have to be used. For this reason, I prefer to use a hotspot question.

2. In **Slide View**, click on the **Flash Movie** button in the **Media Clips** section of the **Insert** ribbon. Navigate to your selected file and then click on **Open**.

3. Add a question and a hotspot.

For the Quizmaker program to be published, you must have an image and a hotspot selected. However, they can be transparent `.gif` files, which can be very small. You can also select **None** in the drop-down menu next to **Feedback** in the ribbon.

4. Switch to **Slide View**. Add the overlay images, objects, and text that you want for your new video, as follows:

5. Publish the video.

How it works...

Essentially we've just tricked the program into thinking that we were creating a quiz, when we were actually creating a new video. However, it does give us the capability to add overlays to our existing video, for using it in a new presentation or anywhere else that we want to.

See also

- ▸ The *Creating a hotspot question* recipe in *Chapter 4, Creating Assessments and Courses with Quizmaker*
- ▸ The *Adding images to a slide* recipe in *Chapter 4, Creating Assessments and Courses with Quizmaker*
- ▸ The *Previewing and publishing your course* recipe in *Chapter 3, Preparing Your Player*

Index

Thank you for buying
Articulate Studio Cookbook

About Packt Publishing

Packt, pronounced 'packed', published its first book "*Mastering phpMyAdmin for Effective MySQL Management*" in April 2004 and subsequently continued to specialize in publishing highly focused books on specific technologies and solutions.

Our books and publications share the experiences of your fellow IT professionals in adapting and customizing today's systems, applications, and frameworks. Our solution based books give you the knowledge and power to customize the software and technologies you're using to get the job done. Packt books are more specific and less general than the IT books you have seen in the past. Our unique business model allows us to bring you more focused information, giving you more of what you need to know, and less of what you don't.

Packt is a modern, yet unique publishing company, which focuses on producing quality, cutting-edge books for communities of developers, administrators, and newbies alike. For more information, please visit our website: www.packtpub.com.

Writing for Packt

We welcome all inquiries from people who are interested in authoring. Book proposals should be sent to author@packtpub.com. If your book idea is still at an early stage and you would like to discuss it first before writing a formal book proposal, contact us; one of our commissioning editors will get in touch with you.

We're not just looking for published authors; if you have strong technical skills but no writing experience, our experienced editors can help you develop a writing career, or simply get some additional reward for your expertise.

Mastering Adobe Captivate 6

ISBN: 978-1-84969-244-1   Paperback: 476 pages

Create professional SCORM-compliant eLearning content with Adobe Captivate

1. Step by step tutorial to build three projects including a demonstration, a simulation and a random SCORM-compliant quiz featuring all possible question slides

2. Enhance your projects by adding interactivity, animations, sound and more

3. Publish your project in a wide variety of formats enabling virtually any desktop and mobile devices to play your e-learning content

Moodle Gradebook

ISBN: 978-1-84951-814-7   Paperback: 128 pages

Set up and customize the gradebook to track student progress through Moodle

1. Use Moodle's powerful gradebook more effectively to monitor and report on the progress of your students

2. Customize the gradebook to calculate and show the information you need

3. Discover new grading features and tracking functions now available in Moodle 2

Please check **www.PacktPub.com** for information on our titles

WordPress for Education

ISBN: 978-1-84951-820-8   Paperback: 144 pages

Create interactive and engaging e-learning websites with WordPress

1. Develop effective e-learning websites that will engage your students

2. Extend the potential of a classroom website with WordPress plugins

3. Create an interactive social network and course management system to enhance student and instructor communication

Mahara ePortfolios: Beginner's Guide

ISBN: 978-1-84951-776-8   Paperback: 328 pages

Create your own ePortfolio and communities of interest within an educational or professional organization

1. A step-by-step approach that takes you through examples with ample screenshots and clear explanations

2. Create, customize, and maintain an impressive personal digital portfolio of web pages and mini websites (collections) with a simple point-and-click interface

3. Create and manage online learning communities and social networks through groups, shared file areas, and forums

Please check **www.PacktPub.com** for information on our titles

www.ingramcontent.com/pod-product-compliance
Lightning Source LLC
LaVergne TN
LVHW062309060326
832902LV00013B/2116